MRYA

W9-AOO-775

SPEAK UP!

A Guide to Having Your Say and Speaking Your Mind

by HALLEY BONDY

with illustrations by
JORDYN BONDS

ZEST BOOKS
San Francisco

ZEST BOOKS

/ Juvenile Non-
fiction > Social Issues > Adolescence
/ Library of Congress data available
/ ISBN: 978-1-936976-76-8 / Art
direction by Adam Grano / Graphic
design by Jimmy Presler

Manufactured in China
SCP 10 9 8 7 6 5 4 3 2 1
4500534587

Connect with Zest!

- zestbooks.net/blog
- zestbooks.net/contests
- twitter.com/zestbooks
- facebook.com/BooksWithATwist

35 Stillman Street, Suite 121
San Francisco, CA 94107

www.zestbooks.net

For my unstoppable niece Sofia, who always speaks her mind.

TABLE
OF
CONTENTS

Introduction	6
Chapter 1: Speaking Up 101	10
Chapter 2: How to Find Your Voice	32
Chapter 3: Your Friends	57
Chapter 4: Bullying	77
Chapter 5: Your Family	96
Chapter 6: Crushes and Relationships	114
Chapter 7: School Life	126
Conclusion: Conquering the World	139
Further Reading	142

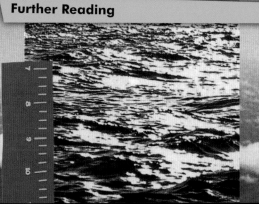

Introduction

Your voice is a truly amazing tool. You use it to sing, shout, share stories, laugh, make friends, get close, answer questions in class, and so much more, every single day! Nobody can read your mind, so your voice is the key to letting the world know who you are and what you want. It is your connection between your brain and the rest of the world.

While your voice is just *screaming* to be heard, far too often, outside forces silence it. There is a lot of pressure on people — and on girls specifically — to say the *right* thing, rather than say the thing that's really on their minds. Sometimes other people — teachers, parents, and kids at school, for example — make you feel like your opinion isn't worth expressing. Other times, girls silence *themselves* through self-doubt.

Maybe someone in your class talked smack about a movie you loved, but you didn't feel comfortable disagreeing with him or her. Maybe a friend "got mad" at you, made fun of you, or ignored you, and you didn't feel like you had the right to defend yourself against them. Or maybe you had trouble disagreeing with your parents about something, even though they were being *totally unfair*. In scenarios like these, it's easy to ignore your feelings and instead get caught up in questions like: "What if I embarrass myself?" "What if people get mad at me?" "What will my friends say?" or worse, "Will I get in trouble?"

We've all had moments when we had something important to say, but we ignored our instincts because we thought what we had to say was too silly, too serious, or that it would have negative consequences. But if you *never* speak up when it's important, your feelings will be buried. And if your feelings are buried, you'll have a tough time identifying what you're actually feeling... and that will make it hard for you to become the person you want to be.

Speak Up will help you... be you. With sample conversations, exercises, and, sure, some advice, you'll learn how to speak up with your friends, when you're in class, when you're at home, and even when you're dealing with crushes. Just like a math textbook, this book starts with the basics and works its way up to speaking-up mastery. *Speak Up* also contains some personal middle school stories from me, your friendly author — after all, I was a middle schooler once, too!

Remember, being truly happy in middle school really isn't about being the smartest or the best-dressed, or having the best phone or the most perfect haircut, even though it feels that way much of the time. In reality, being happy is about sticking to your guns, being yourself, and using your voice to get what you want out of life. After that, the world is your oyster.

CHAPTER 1:
Speaking Up 101

Speaking up applies in a lot of situations, big and small. It can include anything from telling your friend she has spinach in her teeth to speaking to your entire school at an assembly about an important political issue. Speaking up can be simple or hard, but in every case, you are taking a risk, letting yourself be heard, and trying to make change — even if it's teeny tiny change. This chapter covers the basics of speaking up: what it is, what it's not, why it's important, and why it can be so freaking hard sometimes.

Why Speaking Up Matters

Speaking up can serve a lot of purposes.

1. For one, **you can help someone who is having trouble speaking up for herself.** If a new girl is being bullied or is too shy to make friends, helping her out would just *feel* good. Joining the mean girls? You'll definitely regret that.

Here is a fake, but typical conversation between two middle school friends. 'Rachel' is a nice, but *really* unpopular girl in their school.

Adrian: Rachel's sweater was ridiculous today. I told her it looked like a turd.

Anya: Ha. What did she say?

Adrian: She was all, "What's a turd?" Are you serious??

Anya: Wow, she is stupid.

Okay, so that's how the conversation *could* go. But let's imagine for a second that, despite her imperfect fashion sense, Rachel has always been nice to Anya and that Anya kind of likes her. Let's imagine that Rachel's parents don't have a lot of money for clothes, so Adrian is being a little unfair. Saying her sweater was a turd might have been pretty funny, but also *really* mean. It probably made Rachel feel bad, and she already has a hard enough time making friends.

So, now we know how Anya feels for real.

This is what the conversation would have looked like if Anya had spoken up:

Adrian: Rachel's sweater was ridiculous today. I told her it looked like a turd.
Anya: What? Dude… that's mean.
Adrian: Well it's not my fault she dresses like a turd!
Anya: Nobody dresses perfect. Leave her alone. She's nice.
Adrian: Fine, whatever.
Anya: Let's hang out after school?
Adrian: I dunno, are you gonna bring your BFF Rachel?
Anya: Oh yeah, baby, we're getting married, didn't you hear? Meet you at four!
Adrian: Kay.

Anya stood up for someone who needed a hand, and she took the high road in the conversation by saying exactly how she felt. Sure, Adrian might have gotten on her case for a moment, but at the end of the day, Anya owned her point of view, she stood up for what she felt was right, and maybe she even taught Adrian a lesson. They can both move on.

Oh, and if Adrian actually got super mad at Anya for standing her ground… is Adrian really a friend? More on that on page 71.

2. Speaking up will **earn you respect from other kids and adults.** If people know that you're the type of girl who speaks her mind, they'll remember to respect your feelings in the future. If you never speak up, they may not ever know *how* to respect you.

For example:

PE Teacher: You can play catcher because you're a big girl!
Janelle: Okay.
[*One week later*]
PE Teacher: So, you're back on the red team, big gal!
Janelle: Ha. Okay.

This goes on and on and on for the rest of the year. Janelle has to play stupid catcher… forever.

Okay… maybe you're not a big girl, but if you replace the word "big" with anything that you might feel self-conscious about — short, tall, scrawny, or whatever! — it stings just as much. It's not appropriate or professional for a teacher to say things like that, but she probably thought it was friendly and funny. Well, she's wrong, but unfortunately *she won't know that until Janelle speaks up.* Let's flip the script.

PE Teacher: You can play catcher because you're a big girl!
Janelle: (In private) Actually, I don't really like it when people say that.
PE Teacher: Oh, I'm so sorry.
Janelle: Thanks. I just thought I would tell you.
[*One week later*]
PE Teacher: Hey, would you like to play shortstop this week?
I bet you'd be great.
Janelle: Thanks!

Janelle's teacher recognized that she was in the wrong, and she learned to respect Janelle's feelings — but only because Janelle spoke up! If she hadn't, things would have kept going in the same, embarrassing way they'd been going before. By speaking up, Janelle learned that her feelings actually matter to her teacher, and her teacher will try not to embarrass Janelle anymore.

Of course, if this teacher *continued* to be a bully, it would be time for Janelle to tell another adult, like her parents or the principal.

---

3. But most importantly, by speaking up, **you are more likely to get what what you want.** Think of a few women in your life who got what *they* wanted, whether they're your favorite teachers, sports heroes, Beyoncé, your mom... anyone. Chances are, they didn't get to where they are by simply accepting what came their way. They got there after disagreeing with the people who silenced them, by sticking up for themselves, and by saying 'screw it' to others' unfair expectations and judgements! Maybe they made the occasional fool of themselves in the process, but so what? As long as you're not hurting or silencing anyone else, getting what you want is one of the greatest pleasures in life.

Consider this example:

Lauren: I'm going to see the new *Hunger Games* movie tonight!
Mae: Oh... cool.
Lauren: Yeah, I can't wait! My parents are taking me which is sorta lame, but... should be fun.
Mae: It looks like a good one. I hope I get to see it sometime.
Lauren: Yep, see ya!

Okay... you can probably see where this is going. Mae really wanted to see the new *Hunger Games* movie, too, but was too shy to ask. Maybe she was waiting for Lauren to ask her, or perhaps she wasn't sure if it would be okay with her parents. Unfortunately, because she didn't speak up, she'll never know if it were possible to get a ticket.

But, here's what could have happened if Mae had spoken up:

Lauren: I'm going to see the new *Hunger Games* movie tonight!
Mae: Oh... cool.
Lauren: Yeah, I can't wait! My parents are taking me which is sorta lame, but... should be fun
Mae: Hey, if you want to bring a friend, I'm game.
Lauren: Yes! I hadn't thought of that! Let me text my parents and see if they're cool with it!
Mae: I'll ask mine!

There you go. Mae gets a shot at seeing the new *Hunger Games* movie, all because she spoke up. In this scenario, she got what she wanted, but even if she hadn't gotten what she wanted, what's the worst that could have happened? That Lauren says no? That Mae just has to get a ticket on another day? Sure, these outcomes might be uncomfortable and disappointing, but Mae's world won't end. Luckily in this case, she spoke up, and Lauren was happy to follow up with her parents.

Why Speaking Up Is Freaking Hard

Unfortunately, speaking up isn't always easy. Even adults have trouble speaking their minds sometimes. It's scary to take risks and put your feelings on the table for everyone to see. But as hard as it is for adults, it's even harder for middle schoolers.

Why? For one, there's **science.**

It's true: Your brain goes a little haywire in middle school. No matter how smart and amazing and composed you are, nature isn't always your friend when it comes to speaking up.

Right now, your brain is developing at lightning speed, which can cause very powerful, rapidly changing feelings: sadness, anger, embarrassment, fear, happiness, and more. In the meantime, some other useful parts of your brain — logic and organization, for example — are still trying to catch up. So, you've got these big new feelings and not much help making sense of them. It's a bit like unleashing a rabid dog and letting it run completely wild inside your mind for a few years. Eventually it gets tamed, but for now, feelings are going to be pretty intense.

It's time for some truth: Everyone around you is having similar problems. Very few people have an easy time in middle school, and emotional issues have been a staple of the preteen years since the dawn of time! Take a deep breath, hang on, and use as many of the tips in this book as you can to get through it.

To put that same idea another way, this is your brain in middle school:

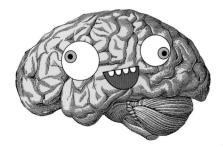

And why do your parents seem like they're from another planet sometimes? Well, among other reasons (brain development can't account for your dad's undying love of Pearl Jam), all of the rapid changes that happened to their brains in middle school have settled. Their brains look like this.

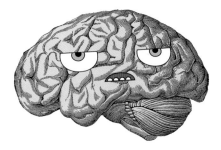

Of course, when you're living with it, it's hard to tell that your brain is going through major changes. But it is important to know that sometimes your growth process may be causing you to feel a bit… extreme about stuff. For example, wearing the wrong shirt is totally life-ruining! Not being invited to a party is the most crushing thing in the world! Your crush not liking you back is the be-all and end-all of your social existence! So speaking up and risking embarrassment (or worse!) can often seem impossible. (The truth: It's not impossible… just a little tricky sometimes.)

Even though your brain sometimes seems to be working against you, it's nice to know that you're not the only one who feels these extreme emotions. Everyone around you is growing and developing too, and experiencing a similar range of roller coaster emotions.

Another reason why it might feel hard to speak up is this: **You're a girl.** This isn't a *correct* way to think, but many girls feel like boys are smarter, stronger, and just… better. Scientifically, we know that isn't true, but for some girls, that sense of inferiority is hard to overcome. This is because our culture still favors boys when it comes to confidence and speaking up, and girls get the message that they ought to be quiet, obedient, and in the background only. As a result, even though they know about feminism and girl power and *want to believe* that women are equal to men, there is still a voice inside their brains that says, "Boys are in charge." Even if it doesn't make sense, it affects how some girls think, how they talk, and how they speak up when boys are involved. (Read more about pressure on girls on page 20.)

Even though boys might often seem bigger, louder, and more confident, they're just as confused as girls are, and their hormones are making them feel just as many wild emotions. Everyone expresses feelings, fears, and personalities differently, so don't assume that someone has it all together just because he looks like he does. You never know what's going on underneath the surface.

One more reason why everything is a little harder in middle school: **Fitting in feels extremely important.** Let's be serious, it *is* important. No matter how many times adults tell you to be yourself and be an individual, it seems crucial to feel like you're not a ridiculous freak in middle school. Your social life is extremely important in your preteen years, which makes it very hard to balance the need to be yourself with the desire to be cool and fit in. It is completely possible, however, to manage those two (often contradictory) responsibilities. Learning to speak up is a great place to start.

Why is it harder for girls?

There is a lot of pressure on preteen girls. Our culture says that you have to be pretty, popular, have a certain kind of body, be a perfect student, and have great style (even though your mom won't always let you buy the clothes you want). Do you ever see a commercial telling a middle school boy how to get the perfect hairstyle? Probably not! Meanwhile, talk is getting more intense surrounding difficult subjects like relationships, hooking up, and drugs, which can be overwhelming when you're confronting them in a real way for the first time.

Plus, kids can be pretty mean in middle school, which doesn't help! Bullying is a full-fledged reality during these years, and not just outright *Mean Girls*–style bullying, but also day-to-day small stuff. If a good friend tells you that your shirt is ugly or out-of-date, it's not exactly like she's throwing you into a locker, but it is still rude, and it still hurts.

Then there's discrimination. As hard as people try to make the world an equal place, it's a fact: Girls are treated differently from boys before and during (and even after) their middle school years. For example, research shows that teachers call on boys in class more often than they call on girls, and they listen to boys even if they're speaking out of turn. If a girl speaks without raising her hand, the teachers tend to punish her for breaking the rules. These subtle inequalities can really affect how girls feel about themselves and how they feel about speaking up.

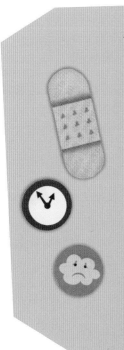

As you read about speaking up, you may feel like you're too young to worry about these things. Some of the most confident, well-spoken women in the world — Oprah Winfrey, Hillary Clinton, Jennifer Lawrence — are much, much older than you, right? Doesn't confidence just come with age? Well, yes, sometimes. Confidence does come with experience: the experience of succeeding, of failing, and of participating in a lot of different friendships and relationships. But even the strongest women in the world remember middle school. While your brain is growing, it is actually forming very lasting memories and ideas about the world, and they could affect the rest of your life! So, now is a great time to start practicing speaking up.

All in all, middle school far from a perfect environment, even at the best of times, but it is entirely possible to be a strong, confident, outspoken girl if you want to be! (For more on confidence turn to page 46). You may have to step out of your comfort zone a little, but getting your voice heard is totally worth it.

Looked at another way, middle school can be a very interesting time for a girl. You're somewhere between being a kid and being a full-fledged teenager. You've still got one foot in your happy, innocent childhood, yet you're ready to start being more independent and grown-up already! There will be no other time in your life like this — so why not make it the best experience possible?

My Story

Middle school was incredibly tough for me. I had a lot of self-esteem problems, and back then (the 1990s), nobody was really talking about mean girls, confidence issues, or the realities of middle school life. I didn't have trouble raising my hand in class, but I did have trouble speaking up if it meant disagreeing with anybody or potentially embarrassing myself. On the outside, I was a good student. I was active in music and sports, and I had a lot of friends. But on the inside, I was suffering so badly that my insecurities escalated into an all-out eating disorder. I lost 30 pounds when my body was supposed to be growing and developing. I went from being slightly chubby to scary-skeletal, and no amount of weight loss was enough for me. I suppressed my feelings (for example, I don't remember expressing anger a single time in middle school), and took out any frustration or pain I felt on my body.

Eventually, I got the help I needed. But to this day, I've never forgotten middle school: the hardships, the obsessions, and the things I could have done differently to make it better.

Years later, I was amazed to learn that many of my friends had similar issues, even if they weren't as extreme as mine. Most of them had body issues of some kind, and all of them were more concerned about how other people saw them than how they felt about themselves. They still remembered the difficulties of middle school like it was yesterday. I couldn't believe it: I wasn't alone. How nice it would have been if we'd known that each of us was going through the same things back then!

I wish I hadn't been so afraid of speaking up in middle school. I wish that I had reached out to my family, my friends, or even the therapist who would see me about the eating disorder. I was so petrified of speaking up about my feelings that I suffered tremendously as a result. If I had only valued my voice a little more, everything could have been different.

Be Gone, Negative Thoughts!

Unfortunately, you can't change the world all by yourself — that is, unless you have a magic wand that makes TV commercials more balanced, girls and boys completely equal all over the world, and bullying nonexistent... and if you have one of those, why haven't you used it yet?! You do have the power, however, to start a revolution right now by focusing on your most powerful tool: your mind.

Yes, there are a lot of outside pressures on young girls. But in some cases, girls put a lot of pressure on themselves without even realizing it. Unlike TV commercials, this is something they can actually control.

A good place to start is to get a grip on the negative thoughts that may run through your head. Sometimes, especially if you are a girl, you may have all kinds of small, everyday bad thoughts. You don't always notice them, and most of the time you don't say them out loud... but they run through your mind lightning fast and seem like total truths. The problem is, if you don't stop and think about them critically, they can hold you back from speaking your mind. They're sort of like annoying sports injuries: If you recognize them early, you can strengthen yourself and recover more quickly. But if you don't, they could eventually incapacitate you!

Here are some examples of negative thoughts that might plague a middle school brain:

- *I want to play, but I suck at this game.*

- *He says my pants are ugly, and he must be right.*

- *Why do we all hate this girl again? Whatever, she deserves it… I think.*

- *My friend says I'm shy, so I'll probably be shy forever.*

- *The teacher didn't call on me, so she definitely hates me.*

- *I think I know a lot about this class discussion, but that guy seems to know everything, so… maybe I don't?*

- *Wow, she likes iPhones? I liked my Android when I got it, but now it seems stupid.*

- *Everyone is looking at my bad haircut. I just want to hide for the rest of the day.*

- *He rejected me, so everyone else will reject me too.*

- *I got that answer wrong, so I'm bad at math.*

- *I'm good at everything in school except history, so I'm not smart or good at school.*

Whew. Anxieties! Okay, let's take a break from that nightmare list for a minute.

Thoughts like these are tough to handle. They show up and take hold of your brain, and for some people, they become obsessions. You can't always prevent these negative thoughts from arriving, but you can chose not to accept them.

Here are eight For-Real Truths that will help you destroy the negative thoughts above:

The For-Real Truths

1. Nothing is forever. There are a lot of "absolutes" and "forevers" on this list which are NOT "absolutes" OR "forevers." People change constantly, and you, too, have the ability to grow and change! If you're not great at a game, for example, you can learn to be better. Everyone has to start somewhere.

2. One person's opinion isn't everything. You'll meet tons of people who will be nice to you, and some others who won't. Some people may think you're shy, while others may think you light up a room. Some people may like your pants, and others may hate them. People are random like that, which is why you should take their negative opinions and actions with a grain of salt.

3. You can't read people's minds. Sometimes, you might read other people incorrectly. Just because a teacher doesn't call on you a few times doesn't mean she hates you. How on earth would you know that? For all you know, she didn't see your hand up. Or she knows you know the answer but wants to call on someone who needs help paying attention. You can't read people's minds, and if you always assume the worst, you'll be too afraid to take risks.

4. Your opinion is just as valid as everybody else's. If somebody feels a certain way, it doesn't override your opinion, no matter how smart or popular or self-assured the other person is. In other words, you have permission to keep liking your Android, even if the coolest girl in school likes her iPhone!

5. Don't let anyone take your feelings away from you. If you feel weird about "hating" a girl, that feeling is worth exploring. Sometimes, it's easier to just go with your friends' opinions, even if they make you feel uncomfortable — but that makes you a follower, not a master of speaking up! Even though it can be uncomfortable, your feelings are worth paying attention to.

6. Nobody is as critical of you as you are. People are mostly self-consumed and have very little time to pick you apart. That's a little freeing, isn't it?

7. One mistake doesn't mean you're doomed. A mistake is just that: a mistake. If you do poorly on one test, that doesn't change who you are or where your abilities lie. Making mistakes is a part of life. Hopefully, you can learn from them and move on.

8. You aren't perfect, and that's okay. Nobody is perfect. You hear that all the time, but it can still be difficult to accept your imperfections and truly be okay with them. If you're not amazing at math but you're great at everything else in school, that's actually pretty normal. Total perfection just isn't possible. (And even if it were, it probably wouldn't be very much fun.)

The Negative Thought Escape Plan

In column one, you'll find the negative thoughts from the list on page 24. In column two, you'll find the For-Real Truths that can talk you out of those negative thoughts. (More than one For-Real Truth may apply.)

Negative thought	Which For-Real Truth can get me out of this?
I think I know a lot about this class discussion, but that guy seems to know everything, so... maybe I don't?	3 and 4
The teacher didn't call on me, so she definitely hates me.	3, 5
He rejected me, so everyone else will too.	1, 2
Everybody is looking at my bad haircut.	3, 5
I failed this math test, so that means I'm bad at math.	7, 8

Got your own negative thoughts? Grab a piece of paper, write them down, and fill in with the For-Real Truths that work for you!

When Not to Speak Up

Of course, speaking up isn't always the most important thing. You don't have to involve yourself in every little fight or class discussion. If you said something every single time you had a thought, you'd never have a chance to listen!

This book shows you how to speak up, but you'll also learn how and when to hold back. Picking your battles is a crucial step in the whole speaking-up process. You should speak up if it helps you or helps someone else... but not if it stirs up needless drama, hurts feelings, or makes you stick your nose where it doesn't belong!

Here are some simple examples to start with.

Should I speak up?

Yes	No
Your friend made fun of you... and took it too far.	Your friend's dress is ugly.
Your mom hurt your feelings.	Your mom got a bad haircut.
You need your teacher's help with homework.	You think your teacher's jokes are dumb.
Your friend is getting bullied.	You heard from Sam who heard from Chloe who saw online that someone you don't know got bullied.

Speaking up isn't about saying something just because it pops into your head — for example, when someone's clothing doesn't look great on her — and it's definitely not about gossiping or spreading fifth-hand rumors. It's about finding that little voice inside your head that says, "This is wrong," or "This is what I really want," and taking action when it feels important.

Reality Check

For some kids, speaking up is a luxury. Not all kids feel like they have the time or freedom to explore their feelings. Some feel overwhelmed with other things — like taking care of their siblings, helping with the family business, or dealing with issues at home. Or maybe they come from a family or culture that doesn't support it.

Even if parts of this book don't feel completely in sync with your life, there are some fundamental truths that apply to everyone: You have feelings, you have needs, and you have wants. You have the right to be in touch with those feelings, and furthermore, you have the right to speak up about them, so long as you're not hurting anyone or getting in serious trouble.

Sometimes, speaking up will just feel like too much of a struggle compared to everything else you have on your plate. However, you can pick and choose the lessons that apply to you, try them out as much as you can now, and carry them with you into adulthood. Your voice is worth hearing!

If you're having trouble figuring out when to speak up and when to hold back, just remember to be kind. Don't use your powers of speaking up to put somebody else down. Speaking your mind is about looking out for yourself, not about concerning yourself with other people's lives and choices. Unless they're hurting you or someone else, live and let live, girl!

So... Who Cares if I Speak Up?

Good question! If you're not swayed by the reasons already mentioned — helping other kids who are being bullied, getting what you want, or gaining respect — how about this: You'll regret it if you don't.

It might sound crazy right now, but you'll remember middle school for the rest of your life. You'll remember the arguments, the mean kids, the embarrassment, the weird things you were completely obsessed with, and how incredibly hard it sometimes was. Most adults, in fact, say their most embarrassing moment happened in middle school. If you feel like you should speak up and you don't, you'll remember it later, and you might regret it. Every day you're making very lasting memories!

Ask an adult the following questions:

• *What was middle school like for you?*

• *What do you remember the most from middle school?*

• *Name a good memory from middle school.*

• *Do you have any regrets about middle school?*

• *What are you hoping my experience will be in middle school?*

Don't forget, though, that you're making good memories, too. You're in a really exciting time in your life when you're seeing things in a new light. In elementary school, kids believe basically everything the grown-ups tell them. Now that you're older, you're beginning to learn that adults aren't always right. You're thinking about the world around you in totally new ways, and you're starting to care more about issues outside of your everyday life, like human rights, poverty, or the environment. You're developing deeper friendships, reading more advanced books, and asking more complicated questions.

You're beginning, essentially, to be yourself, and the most important thing in middle school is to be the best you possible.

CHAPTER 2:
How to Find Your Voice

Before you speak up, you have to find your voice. Finding your voice basically means getting in touch with how you really feel, no matter what the rest of the world is saying. For some people, this is easier said than done. In middle school, you are growing and changing every day, and the pressure is on from all sides. How can you know what you're feeling, why, and what to do about it? This chapter will help show you the way!

Who Are You?

"Who are you?" It sounds like a simple question: You're you, of course! You have a name, an address, a family, favorite classes, hobbies, favorite TV shows, and maybe a pet. All of these facts are really important parts of who you are.

But there is a whole lot more to you, too. When you have a conversation, do you only talk about your name and address and classes and facts like these over and over again? No! You talk about everything, and when you do, you express feelings, thoughts, personality traits, confidence, humor, and all the little things that add up to make you unique. So, the answer to the question, "Who are you?" is actually very complicated.

Once again, this is a tough question for adults, but an even tougher one for middle schoolers. Your brain is still forming itself (see page 17), so the answer to "Who are you?" isn't completely formed, either.

But there is definitely a very strong version of you that is developing all the time. Finding and listening to her is the key to understanding who you are.

So, let's start with a tried-and-true exercise.

The "Who Am I?" Exercise

Let the answers come to you. Don't think too hard — just answer with the first thing that comes to mind!

1. What I like most about myself is…

2. Something I could improve on is…

3. I would like to tell my parents that…

4. Something that gets on my nerves is…

5. My favorite thing to do in the world is…

6. The thing I wish for the most in the world is…

7. I'm very grateful that…

8. When I get embarrassed, I…

9. When I do something I'm proud of, I…

See, you're not just a collection of facts. You have opinions and feelings. You bring unique ideas to the table, and you have a particular way of handling problems. Chances are, your answers to the questions above look different from your friends' or siblings' answers — because they're not you. You view the world in a totally different way from them. That's what makes you *you*.

The Truth About Feelings

Feelings are very difficult topics in middle school. Again, your brain is on fire, and you are wedged between being a kid and being a teenager. One minute, you might feel totally mature, like you understand the reasoning behind everything you're feeling. The next minute, you may burst into tears like you did in elementary school. Sometimes, it seems proper not to show any emotion, even when you feel like a big mess inside. Other times, you might find yourself acting way more amped up than anyone else in the room. Your feelings can take you up and down so fast it'll make your head spin!

You're already familiar with the toll of such emotions as sadness, anger, fear, peace, happiness, etc. But here are some important things to bear in mind about those feelings that might help you put them in perspective and clear the path to speaking your mind.

1. Feelings aren't always rational or fair. Sometimes, you may feel angry, sad, or happy without really understanding why. For example, your mom gives you a shirt for your birthday, and even though it's a nice shirt and you asked for the shirt last week, you're suddenly angry that it's not a gift card. This isn't necessarily fair to your mom — she had no idea! — but your feelings are your feelings and you can't always control them. That's part of being human.

2. Your feelings aren't a choice, but your actions are. Feelings of happiness, sadness, anger, jealousy, etc., will come up whether you want them to or not, and again, they might not be fair or rational. However, just because you feel a certain way, that doesn't mean that everyone can see that feeling written on your forehead or that you must share it. You get to pick and choose which feelings you want to act on and how to express [them...] [You might decide], for example, that you're angry [at your mom to]day, but you can choose to tell [...] her know later that you'd like a [...]

[...] [fe]elings, whether they're pleasant [... You mig]ht feel really angry with a friend [because s]he did something really terrible, [... You might feel like your world is [... reje]cts you, but you'll get over that, [... th]e best day ever (ever!) at a local [... eventually. The best thing to do [... a]nd let them run their course. Try

4. You can feel many different ways about the same thing.
Feelings aren't black and white. You can feel good about some parts of something and bad about other parts. So, for example, maybe you like *Minecraft* but you find parts of it boring or lame, and actually, you like other games a lot better. That doesn't mean you don't like *Minecraft*; you just have many feelings about it. That's how feelings usually are: mixed. You don't have to feel one way or the other about stuff. Mixed feelings are valid feelings!

5. Sometimes you think you feel one way, when you really feel another. Some people gossip when they're actually deeply jealous on the inside. Or they bully people because they are uncomfortable with themselves and they want to put all the negative attention on someone else. Or they might think they're happy because someone they admire complimented them on their new jeans, but really they're proud of themselves for choosing the jeans all on their own. Whenever you can remember to, check in with yourself and ask, "How do I really feel?" Then decide what to do from there!

The "How Do I Really Feel?" Exercise

Think about an issue that upset you in the last year. Maybe a friend, a teacher, a parent, or a sibling did something, or continues to do something, that makes you mad, sad, or embarrassed. Think hard about that incident for a few minutes, even if it's tough, and let your emotions run free (nobody's looking!). Then, try to fill in as many blanks as you can below (use another piece of paper if you want to do this exercise more than once), and remember that there are no wrong answers — because feelings don't always make sense!

I feel _____ when you _____ .

I also feel _____ , _____ , and _____ ...

but mostly I feel _____ .

For the last sentence below, think about the best course of action to deal with your feelings in an ideal world. Is it to: Tell an adult? Talk about it after school? Tell the person in private? Or is it most appropriate to do nothing?

I should deal with it by _____ .

You vs. the World

In order to speak your mind, you need to have a pretty good idea of who you are. If you are overly concerned with what the rest of the world thinks, that will tend to get in the way of knowing your own mind and speaking up on your own behalf.

Imagine an iPad. The screen shines and the technology inside is very powerful. An iPad can even do cool stuff like control the TV and the lights.

Okay, now let's put a cover on the iPad while it's still on. Suddenly, the patch of light from the screen is missing. We can't even see the awesome features of the iPad anymore because, well, they're covered. We *know* there's a glowing screen under there (until it switches off, anyway), but it's not visible to the world.

Now, let's bring it back to you. If you're only concerned with what everyone else thinks of you, your best parts can get covered up by everyone else's beliefs and feelings. Just like the covered iPad screen, you won't be able to share your best features with the world.

Most people are at least a little concerned about what other people think of them, and sometimes that's a good thing. You should care about stuff like being kind to people, doing your homework, being a good sibling, behaving in class, "doing unto others as you would have them do unto you"… in other words, all the basic rules. The goal is to find a good balance: Be a kind, caring person, but also make sure you express yourself when things are unfair, when you don't feel heard, or when you or somebody else needs help.

Nobody can make you less awesome on the inside. But other people can affect how you feel about yourself and how much of your awesome self you share with the world. The idea is not to let the opinions of other people completely consume you — or switch you off.

Here's an Idea…
Do a completely random chore around the house. At first this exercise might sound like the complete opposite of fun, but give it a chance. Do a chore at home on your own. It has to be something you've never done before and something your parents haven't asked you to do. The chore should be something small and reasonable, like wiping down your kitchen counters or arranging a bookshelf by color, instead of something totally overwhelming, like reorganizing the entire garage. Taking on a new task on your own is a great way to get in touch with your individuality. Suddenly, you are a contributor in the house, you have ideas about how your surroundings should look, and you have some control over the space you live in. And, as an added bonus, your family will be happily surprised at your cleaning initiative!

Enemy Territory

In the world of middle school, you are battling against a lot of enemy behaviors, which are basically things that people do and say to make you feel bad. This doesn't mean the perpetrators are all bad people, mind you, or even that they're aware of what they're doing while they're doing it, but their behavior can still have a very damaging effect.

If you don't recognize the behavior for what it is — if you buy into it or constantly try to adapt to it — then the enemy behaviors might eclipse your real feelings.

Here's a guide to handling the worst enemy behaviors:

1. Cold and distant

What it looks like: It's when someone acts like they're not interested in hanging out with you or listening to what you have to say, even though you've done nothing wrong to them.

Potential damage: It makes you feel like you are not important. It may lead you to apologize for stuff you didn't do or go out of your way to make someone happy when, in reality, these efforts are futile.

The reality: This person will either come around or they won't, but it is more than likely that their behavior has nothing to do with you personally. They probably handle everyone the same way, not just you, and there's nothing you can do to stop them from being cold and distant when they want to be.

How to handle it: Accept that it's their problem, not yours; let it go, and be yourself! That's the best way to make this enemy behavior insignificant.

2. Mr. or Ms. Expert

What it looks like: It's when a classmate knows everything about clothes, the latest music and movies, and insults other people's opinions and knowledge about these things. Hey, they even know more about you than you do.

Potential damage: You might actually start to believe this jerk! Suddenly your knowledge or opinions start to feel meaningless or incorrect.

The reality: Nobody is a true expert on everything. You are entitled to your own feelings, and remember that just because someone seems confident in their knowledge, it doesn't mean they're right.

How to handle it: If you have your own opinion or a different version of someone else's "facts," you can nicely tell Mr. or Mrs. Expert that you disagree. However, don't be disheartened if they don't come around to your side... after all, he or she is an "expert"!

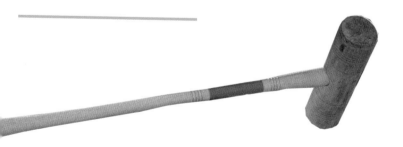

3. Classic bullying

What it looks like: Bullying takes many forms. It can occur in class, in the halls, or even online. It can be verbal or physical. But whatever its form, it causes real harm.

Potential damage: You may feel powerless and start to believe the bully's insults. You may feel like you have to avoid certain classes or areas of the cafeteria.

The reality: A bully likely has personal issues that have nothing to do with you. You have every right to be angry if you are being bullied, and every right to feel safe everywhere in school.

How to handle it: If bullying behavior is making you or someone close to you feel uncomfortable or unsafe, tell a teacher, guidance counselor, or another adult (read more on page 86).

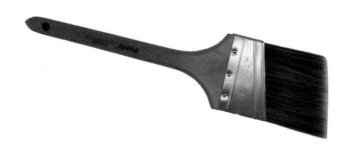

4. Bloodsucking behavior... like a vampire! (But not the Edward Cullen kind.)

What it looks like: It's when someone is very demanding of your time and energy. They text and e-mail too much, or they want to hang out all the time. Sometimes they get angry with you when you don't want to spend time with or talk to them, even though you've proven yourself to be a good friend dozens of times already.

Potential damage: You might run around in circles trying to appease this kind of behavior. You may do things that feel uncomfortable, such as sending texts more than you're allowed to, in order to keep up with this person's demands. In the worst instances, you may find yourself totally unhappy and embroiled in a relationship or friendship that's not even fun or good for you anymore.

The reality: You will never appease a vampire! Their thirst is unquenchable! You are going to drive yourself up the wall if you indulge this kind of behavior.

How to handle it: Do your thing, and let the vampire realize that you're a separate person, not a source of food. If their behavior becomes overwhelming, you should distance yourself.

Confidence

You probably hear the word "confidence" a lot. Your parents and teachers throw it around all the time, while advertisers and celebrities use it on TV, in magazines, and whenever the cameras are rolling. "Make confidence the must-have accessory!" said Google in a 2014 YouTube campaign. "Confidence is the only key [to beauty]!" said Emma Stone in an interview with *People*. "Strong Lasting Makeup for Strong, Confident Women," said Maybelline about its recent lines of eye makeup, blushes, and lipsticks. This is a great sign of progress: Only a generation ago, the word "confidence" wasn't heard anywhere when it came to young girls. But these days, it's used so often and in so many ways that some people have forgotten what the word *really* means.

To quote the great Emma Stone, confidence is the key, especially when it comes to speaking your mind. But what is confidence, really? What does it look like? How does it lead to speaking up?

In short, confidence is a person's ability to believe in herself and her feelings, despite all of the noise around her. Even if her friend doesn't agree with her, even if her teacher tells her she's wrong, even if the ads on TV tell her to be different from who she is, a confident person remains in touch with her own thoughts, feelings, and opinions. Basically, in a brain that is crowded with other people's voices, her voice is still the strongest of them all.

If you have confidence in yourself, your chances of speaking up are much higher. After all, it's a lot easier to speak your mind when you really believe in the thing you're speaking up *for*.

So, think of a position that you are totally, 100 percent sure of. For example: Chocolate tastes awesome. It's hard to imagine a world where anyone would disagree with that, but try to imagine it anyway. This is what that conversation might sound like.

You: Chocolate rules.

Friend: No, you're crazy.

You: How am I crazy? Chocolate is the best!

Friend: Nobody thinks that! You're so weird!

You: I don't really care if you think I'm weird. I think chocolate is awesome, and that's how I feel.

Friend: Whatevs, crazypants.

Now, swap chocolate with something a little more... difficult. For example, maybe you're the only one of your friends who likes the *Divergent* series. You should still approach it with the same 100 percent attitude you showed when you were debating chocolate.

You: I love the *Divergent* series.

Friend: Lame. Nerd. Sorry Not Sorry.

You: *Divergent* is amazing!

Friend: Not at *all*! Omg, I can't believe you like it.

You: Like it? I *love* it! You should give it a try!

Now... let's ramp this up to an *even more* difficult scene, where you disagree with your friend about an argument she is having with someone else.

Friend: I'm so mad at [so and so] right now. Can you believe what she said?

You: I get that you're mad, but in the end it's not that big of a deal. She's great, and you're best friends!

Friend: Are you serious? Did you hear what she said to me?

You: Sorry, I just don't see it as a big deal and I don't think you should fight about it.

Friend: 'Kay, whatever.

You: We'll agree to disagree... but I wish you would make up.

In this case, your friend had a very intense reaction to your opinion about the fight. If you were less confident in your opinion, you may have backpedaled and agreed with your friend for no reason. But, because you approached your opinion with confidence, you spoke out in favor of your friend, *and* in favor of peace. That's something to be proud of!

All of this sounds easy on paper, but how do you get to a place where you feel totally, chocolate-level sure about a thing? It's very hard to be completely certain about something when the rest of the world won't necessarily agree. Second-guessing yourself is natural, and everybody does it, but there are a few tactics you can use to become more confident:

1. Fake it until you make it. If you just fake being confident, sometimes it can lead to really feeling confident in a meaningful way. Pretending gives you practice, and you may find out that the world won't fall apart when you speak up. In the words of Facebook executive Sheryl Sandberg (who instructs adult women on speaking up), ask yourself the question, "What would you do if you weren't afraid?" Then do it!

2. Cut the apologies. Girls tend to apologize more than boys, even over stupid stuff. We say "sorry" when we have an opinion, we say "sorry" when we ask for things we need, or worse, we say "sorry" when someone else bumps into us or gets in our way. We also start sentences with apology-like phrases, such as, "I'm not good at this, but…", or "I may not know what I'm talking about, but…" Count how many times you apologize in one day, and keep track of why. Is an apology really necessary in those situations, or is it just a reflex? Are you really doing something wrong, or are you just apologizing out of habit?

3. Confident body, confident mind. Something as simple as changing your body posture might help your confidence. Simple actions like sitting up straight and taking up more space with your body are scientifically proven to boost your self-image. Walk with your head up, and it gets your confidence up!

4. Leave those questions at the door. A lot of people ask themselves so many questions before they speak up: Am I really right? Am I the correct person to do this? Is it going to hurt people's feelings? Am I going to look stupid? Unfortunately, if you get caught up in these doubts, they could shatter your confidence. You can't always stop these questions in their tracks, but remember to look at them critically instead of just accepting them.

5. Sometimes, uncertainty is okay! Let's say you're not 100 percent sure that you disagree with your friends' fight or that you like the *Divergent* series. Maybe you only sort of disagree with the fight between your friends, or maybe you only like the first installment of *Divergent*. Hey, that's still a feeling, isn't it? You can be chocolate-confident about having mixed feelings, too!

Believe it or not, "I'm not sure if I agree," "I don't know how I feel about it," or "I see many different sides to this" can all be confident statements, too. In the end, if you believe in what you're saying, it will show.

Confidence vs. Arrogance

Nobody wants to be a show-off, and nobody wants to be crazy-confident in something only to regret it later on. However, very often girls are so afraid of looking arrogant, mean, or difficult that it holds them back from being confident at all.

Here is a breakdown of what arrogance is and isn't:

Arrogance is...	Arrogance isn't...
Deliberately using your talents or knowledge to put people down.	Raising your hand often.
Breaking rules just because you can.	Telling a friend, teacher, or parent that you disagree with him or her.
Saying you're perfect (when no one is).	Going after a challenge, like auditioning for a school play or running for student government.
Taking credit for something that you didn't do.	Being proud of your achievements.
Refusing to admit you may be wrong.	Feeling a certain way (you can feel however you want: jealous, angry, competitive, proud ... it's just a feeling!).

My Story

When I was in the 8th grade, a family member threw a high school party at my house while my parents were away. It was a pretty small party, but on this particular weekend my parents had left the house in the care of their friend, Olivia.* At some late night hour, the music started pounding and a dozen or so high-school kids poured in while we were trying to sleep. When I realized what was happening, more than anything, I felt really sorry for Olivia. She was pretty young herself, and she was just trying to have a calm weekend and do a favor for my parents.

So, what did I do? I marched downstairs (in my dorky pajamas) and boldly turned down the music. I announced something along the lines of, "Be quiet, keep it down, Olivia is trying to sleep!" It was like a record-scratch moment in movies. I watched in horror as these high school kids stared at me in silence, then smiled... and not in a nice way. Some of them laughed, some of them clearly felt sorry for me, but nobody had any intention of turning down the music.

I felt ridiculous. To them, I was nothing more than a goofy little girl in her matching pajamas who was trying to ruin their good time — and clearly, I had failed. Humiliated, I walked upstairs and tried to sleep through the bass. The party died down pretty quickly after that. Olivia later told my parents about it, of course, and they were not happy.

For a long time, I considered that moment a great humiliation and nothing else. Okay, it was pretty embarrassing standing in my pajamas in front of the older kids — who were the kings and queens of high school, as far as I was concerned. I had spoken up, and it hadn't worked. But, while it may not have been my coolest moment, it's actually pretty clear that they were all being jerks, that Olivia wasn't prepared to deal with the situation, and that I did my very best to do what was right — which was pretty brave for a kid who didn't speak up much. Now, I see it as a proud moment, matching PJs and all.

* name has been changed

QUIZ: Which inspiring celebrity are you?

1. I'm best at...

A. Performing and/or arts.	B. School and getting good grades.
C. Sports.	D. All of the above!

2. I like to dress...

A. Super fashionably and up-to-date.	B. Inconspicuously.
C. Comfortably.	D. In as many different styles as possible!

3. Out of my friends, I am...

A. The funny one.	B. The smart one.
C. The tomboy.	D. All of the above!

4) When it comes to talking to new people, I am...

A. Outgoing — especially when you're being creative.	B. Polite and a little shy.
C. Rough around the edges, but fun.	D. A loudmouth, and proud of it!

5) My favorite animal is...

A. A peacock.	B. A cat.
C. A lion.	D. All of the above? Is that possible?

SPEAK UP!

6) What is your idea of the perfect weekend?	
A. Dance party!	B. Staying home with the family.
C. A sleepover with a few friends.	D. Traveling to a totally new place.

7) I wish I could learn to...	
A. Develop the perfect singing voice.	B. Build my own supercomputer
C. Run faster than anyone in the world.	D. All of the above, of course!

Mostly A's

You are: Beyoncé! You are most definitely an amazing lady. You're already fun to be around, but you really shine when you're being artistic. You stand out in a room and you love the attention, but the attention needs to be on your terms. You're kind and nurturing, but you don't let people walk all over you. In the end, you make your own choices.

Mostly B's

You are: Emma Watson! You're not a huge fan of the spotlight — but you actually look great in it! Sometimes it takes you a little time to warm up to people, but that can be a very strong place to be. You don't become fast friends with people who will annoy or hurt you, and you don't always hop aboard the latest trend just because other people are following it. You prefer getting good grades to getting the perfect shoes — and guess what, shoes won't get you into a good college!

Mostly C's

You are: Alex Morgan! You're probably an athlete — or at the very least, you're competitive. You go for what you want, and you're not afraid of a little challenge. Some people might be intimidated by your drive and ambition, but you're just super focused. Inside, you're a softie. You have a lot of friends whom you care about deeply, and you don't have any time for drama!

Mostly D's

You are: Jennifer Lawrence! People love you. You're a social butterfly and you love to be a part of school activities. Your (many) friends think you're a ridiculous amount of fun. You're curious and full of energy. Secretly, you also take your talents and hobbies very seriously, and you have a wide range of them. At the very least, you'll try anything once! Also, if anyone messes with you, you take the high road. There are plenty of other friends to choose from.

A good mix of A's, B's, C's and D's

You're: BeyEmmAlexJen!... or some kind of superhero combination of all these amazing ladies! You're complex and you love to dabble in any area that interests you. You're smart, adventurous, competitive, and creative. You have a lot of friends, but you enjoy the occasional quiet time, too. You don't like to tie yourself down to one social group. Even though school can be tough sometimes, you know that everything you learn will help you at some point in your life.

When Speaking Up Backfires

So, you spoke up, and it didn't go as planned. Maybe nobody listened to you, or you were laughed at, or you started a conflict you never meant to start — or worse, you got in trouble. There's no denying that a backfire can make you totally miserable and regret ever speaking up to begin with. It can also feel completely humiliating.

The Big H — humiliation — is one of the most obvious risks of speaking up. It's really, really, really hard to put yourself out there, only to feel foolish or exposed as a result. However, there are a few important things to remember when you start to fall into a shame slump.

1. Just because speaking up didn't work out, that doesn't mean you were wrong. Remember the feelings rule from page 26, "Don't let anyone take your feelings away from you"? That rule also applies here. Just because you spoke up and people didn't react the way you wanted them to doesn't mean you were wrong to speak up. Sometimes, it just means that there is a difference of opinion, which can be hard to deal with, but it's nothing to feel embarrassed about.

2. You did the right thing. Be proud of yourself! Even if it didn't work out the way you wanted it to, you can stand tall knowing that you did what was right.

3. The most important people in history spoke up, and sometimes, it didn't work out for them, either. People thought Einstein was crazy. Malala Yousafzai's life was threatened when she spoke out for Pakistani women. If either of these figures had let humiliation consume them during those moments, they wouldn't be the people we know today.

4. Ask yourself: Are you angry? It's a strange reflex, but sometimes, when we're really angry at someone for failing us, we turn those feelings on ourselves and feel embarrassed instead. In some ways, it's easier to feel embarrassed. Being mad at someone is harder and more complicated. For example, let's say your friend is late to meet up, and you have been waiting for an hour. Maybe you feel embarrassed that you've been waiting for so long, like a dog waiting at a door. But really, are you just mad at your friend for being late? You certainly have the right to be!

5. It's really, truly not the end of the world. People forget things a lot faster than you think. While you may carry embarrassment with you for a while, chances are that in a few days nobody else will even remember what happened. If they do, they probably need to get a life.

CHAPTER 3:
Your Friends

Friends are the best. They are a source of joy, laughter, conversation, creativity, and relief during a difficult school day. Your friends are there to celebrate with you when you're feeling good, comfort you when you're feeling bad, and goof around with you when you're feeling silly.

But sometimes, things can get tough with friends — especially in middle school. Most of the time you'll have the most fun ever, but sometimes you'll find yourself in a minefield of arguments, competition, insecurity, and general craziness. It's easy to lose your voice. How do you speak up when your brain and hormones are changing, when your tastes are changing, when the social hierarchy is changing… when everything is changing?

This chapter is all about handling friendship pitfalls and speaking your mind… even when your friends aren't making it easy!

Friends are #1 in Middle School!

In middle school, friends are #1. In one survey, middle schoolers put their social lives above everything else, including school, family, and activities. Maybe this isn't necessarily true for you, but it makes sense that some middle schoolers would feel this way. Middle schoolers feel more independent from their parents than ever before. For the first time, they're developing ideas, clothing and music tastes, and political views that might be different from their parents'. This is all a natural part of growing up, even if your folks don't get it.

If you aren't relying on your family for guidance about how to act, dress, date, and eat, then where do you go? Most middle schoolers turn to their friends. They start to look to them for guidance on everything from the everyday to the super important: What should I wear? What music should I listen to? What shows are my friends watching? Does he or she think I'm pretty enough? How much should I study? Is it better to take the bus to school or get a ride from my parents? What activities should I be involved in? Is the guy I like cool enough?

You might not find yourself asking these questions in so many words, but if you think about it, your friends' opinions probably matter a lot — but that can be confusing when it comes to speaking up. If your friends happen to be very assertive, your opinions and needs may get lost or silenced. Sure, friends may be #1 to you, but your voice should rank even higher than that... whatever number that is!

Disagreeing Is Okay

Sometimes, you totally agree with your friends, no questions asked. Having things in common — like taste in music and movies, activities you're passionate about, and jokes that crack you up — is probably one of the reasons why you're friends in the first place.

The time will come, however, when you and your friends will disagree about something. A lot of the time you'll just shrug your shoulders and move on. Who cares if she thinks cheese pizza is the best pizza and you can't live without pepperoni? You're both still eating pizza, and it's delicious! But disagreements can be more complicated. They can lead to a fight, and if you're not careful, you may wind up going along with something you don't believe in, just to keep the peace.

When a disagreement comes up with a friend, it's important to remember a fundamental rule: People don't always agree with each other. Two separate people can't agree on every little thing. In fact, that's impossible! After all, you're two different people!

However, a disagreement doesn't mean that you stop being friends, that you don't love each other, or that the friend will dislike you permanently because of it.

Here are three quick examples of disagreements between two friends, Angela and Maria:

Example 1:

Angela: Wanna come to my house this week?
Maria: No, not this week. Not really in the mood for a sleepover.
Angela: All right, let me know when you are.

Example 2:

Maria: I want to sit in the back of the bus.
Angela: I like the front better.
Maria: Fine, we'll sit in the front.

Example 3:

Angela: I'm gonna take French this year. Will you take it with me?
Maria: No, I like Italian better, sorry.
Angela: Boo. I'll miss you.

In all three of these short conversations, both girls spoke up about what they wanted, and they didn't share the same opinion. Neither Angela nor Maria got what they wanted out of the deal each time, but they're still friends, and they still clearly care about and like each other. They didn't let a few small things get in the way of that.

Speaking up and disagreeing with a friend doesn't have to shatter a good, strong friendship! If you both give a little, you can still have a happy, healthy relationship.

What are some of the areas where you really value your friends' opinions? Take a few minutes to think about it and list some of the areas where you look to your friends for answers to your questions. Examples: "How should I dress?" or "What app should I download?

The Power of Compromise

Striking a compromise is a great way to speak up and to solve a disagreement with a friend. Sometimes, a willingness to compromise is mistaken for a weakness: People can think that if you're not fighting to get your way, you're the weak one in the argument. Not true! Using the power of compromise shows maturity and strength. Besides, there is a major difference between fighting, compromising, and caving in, and they all have different results:

Fighting is using strong words or maybe no words (aka the silent treatment) to express your viewpoint. In this case, one or both people speak up about what they want, but they don't come to an agreement or solve the problem. Fighting is usually more about making yourself heard than it is about making things better. (More on fighting on page 64.)

Compromising is coming to an agreement that works for both people. The people involved may not get everything they want out of the deal, but both voices are heard and respected. Once a compromise is reached, both people can move on from the problem.

Caving in is coming to an agreement, but only after one person gives in to the other person's demands. One person ends up getting everything she wants while the other person gets a raw deal!

Out of the options above, doesn't compromising sound the best? Fighting isn't fun for anyone, and it doesn't usually lead to the best results, either. On the other hand, if you cave in all the time, your voice won't be heard and you'll probably start feeling really frustrated. So, how do you compromise?

In order to compromise, you have to look at a problem logically, find a solution, and then propose that solution to your friend.

Let's take the bus seat example from page 60.

In this example, Angela and Maria fight:

Maria: I want to sit in the back of the bus.
Angela: I like the front better.
Maria: We always do what you want!
Angela: Oh my God, stop whining!
Maria: Forget it. You go to the front, I'll go to the back.
Angela: Fine.

Yikes. Hopefully, choosing a seat on the bus won't be the end of their friendship! In this example, it's clear that both girls spoke up... but the result wasn't exactly a good one.

If a disagreement is reaching a stalemate and you can't seem to find a way to compromise, remember these simple words: We can agree to disagree. It's one of the oldest and most reliable ways to end a disagreement!

In the next example, Angela caves in:

Maria: I want to sit in the back of the bus.
Angela: I like the front better.
Maria: Too bad. We're sitting in the back from now on.
Angela: (sighs) Okay, fine. I guess I don't care.

That example is sort of sad, because Angela just caved in without speaking up for herself. She'll have to sit in the back of the bus, even though she really does like the front better.

In this last example, Angela suggests a compromise:

Maria: I want to sit in the back of the bus.
Angela: I like the front better.
Maria: Back!
Angela: Okay… let's sit in the back today, and then sit in the front tomorrow.
Maria: Okay.

Hooray! Here, Angela offered a simple compromise, and Maria agreed. They both still get to sit where they want to… just not every day of the week. Plus, both of their opinions were heard and respected.

Speaking Up in a Friend Fight

Of course, a compromise isn't always possible. A friend may be stubborn or a situation may get way too emotional for a peaceful agreement. In these cases, a fight may break out, whether you want one or not!

During a fight with a friend, speaking up can get complicated. How do you speak up when someone just won't listen to reason? How do you speak up when someone is yelling at you? How do you speak up when a friend won't even talk to you?

Unfortunately, there's no exact science to speaking up for yourself in a fight, because at the end of the day, there's no way to predict how things will turn out. One friend may see the error of her ways after a simple apology or after some time has passed, while another friend may keep fighting no matter what you say. However the fight turns out, if you speak up for yourself, you will walk away from it with your head high, and you'll command respect from your friend in the future.

Here are some dos and don'ts for speaking up in a fight.

 **Speaking up should never turn violent!** Physical fighting is never okay, no matter how mad you are. Not only could you get hurt, but you could get in major trouble. If you feel a physical fight brewing, leave immediately and find an adult.

Do:

Pick your battles. Ask yourself: Is this fight worth the drama? Maybe the fight is way too petty to get involved in or you're really not interested in working things out. If you walk away from a silly fight, that's not cowardice. In fact, it's just like speaking up. You're sending the message that you are bigger than the fight.

Get your viewpoint across. Make sure your friend is aware of your viewpoint on the issue. There's nothing worse than fighting when people totally don't understand why you're upset or where you're coming from. Be clear about what you want and why you want it.

Stay true to yourself. If you know you're right, don't pretend you agree with your friend in order to make things okay. (That's caving in!) Stick to your true stance. Having an opinion you really believe in is something to be proud of!

Own up. If you know you've done something wrong, it is a very brave thing to admit it and apologize. Apologizing for what you know you've done wrong may also end a fight earlier.

Learn to let go. Sometimes, a fight just needs a little breathing room. Speaking up is great, but if you talk about the fight constantly when you're both in distress, things may actually get worse. You just need to give yourselves time and space for all the tough emotions to cool off before you try speaking up again.

Don't:

Try to control your friend with words. You can't predict how a friend will react. If you speak up with the intention of making your friend forgive you or making your friend apologize, the fight may only get worse. You can't control other people's reactions, so don't even try.

Apologize for things you didn't do. When a friend is mad, it can be easy to jump up and apologize right away — even if you don't mean it. However, that kind of reaction won't necessarily make you feel great later on, and it sends the message to your friend that you're always willing to take blame you don't deserve.

A good alternative is to apologize for some things but not others. For example, "I am truly sorry for how I've been acting during the fight — but I still don't think what I did was wrong."

Tolerate abusive behavior. Bullying or mental abuse is never okay, no matter what you did. Read more about speaking up against bullying and abuse in Chapter 4.

Speaking Up For an Even Better Friendship

So far, this chapter has been all about disagreements, fights, and standing up for your beliefs in difficult situations. But what about speaking up in order to make friendships stronger and more fun? It's easy to get complacent with a good friend. But all strong friendships need a little work — and a little speaking up!

Here's how to speak up to better your friendship:

Suggest new stuff, often. If you and your friend have been doing the same stuff over and over again, suggest something different! Go to the other person's house for a change. Watch a different movie. Play a different game. To keep things interesting, you may to have to voice some new ideas.

Get out of your comfort zone. Start a dance party in your room! Build a fort or run around the yard like you used to do when you were little! Hold a limbo contest! Leave your inhibitions at the door! When you're hanging out with a friend, being silly with each other can bring you even closer and create some of the best memories on the planet. Chances are, you'll remember letting loose much more clearly than you'll remember the millionth time you watched *Frozen* together.

Talk about things that bother you. Calmly. You don't have to fight with a friend to talk about something that bothers you about your friendship. In fact, sometimes it's better to voice your opinion when you're not in the heat of a fight. Maybe you and your friend fight all the time, and that bothers you. Talk it out calmly and work out some ways to prevent fights in the future.

Tell your friends you care about them. Once in a while it's nice to tune in with your friends and tell them that you love them — or at least that you like them a whole lot! Your openness may strengthen your friendship, and make room for even more fun stuff.

Reach out when your friend is feeling low. If your friend is having a rough time, don't wait around for her to tell you. Reach out and ask, "How are you? Do you need to talk?" It could make a huge difference for her. Plus, your friend will know that you sincerely care.

If you're worried, talk to an adult. If you're really worried about a friend and you don't know what steps to take, tell an adult. For example, if your friend is engaging in dangerous behavior or if he or she is acting depressed or totally different from usual, talk to your friend's parents, your parents, or a guidance counselor at school.

Speaking Up Against Peer Pressure

"Peer pressure" is one of those phrases that is thrown around so much you almost don't hear the words anymore. But even though it is discussed nonstop by adults, peer pressure is still a very real thing.

In middle school, things like drugs, alcohol, sex, and other potential risks are on the forefront of many preteen minds. Some kids are more interested in this stuff than others. (And some kids have more experience than others, too.) As you read on page 58, middle schoolers depend a lot on their friends for guidance, so sometimes kids are lured into activities they don't exactly want to do or things that they're not ready for. This is the true meaning of peer pressure, and if you don't speak out against it, you may wind up doing something you'll regret.

Remember, you don't have to do anything you don't feel like doing. If it makes you uncomfortable, say no! You have the rest of your life to try new things. In the meantime, here's how to say no to a peer pressurer (which is a phrase we just made up).

Try a simple "no thanks." You don't owe anyone an explanation, and you don't have to put somebody else down in order to say no. This isn't an Oscar speech — it doesn't have to be long and eloquent — it's a simple "no thanks." Try it!

Stick to it. A true peer pressurer will probably try to convince you once or twice before they back down. Stick to "no thanks" and they should eventually give up.

Keep explanations brief, firm, and final. If you feel like you have to explain yourself, don't give the peer pressurer anything to work with. If you say, "I don't want my mom to know," they might retort with, "She won't find out!" But if you say, "I'm just not interested, period," how can a peer pressurer argue with that?

Walk away. If the peer pressurer won't stop, leave. If they've pushed it to this point, they're in official bully territory, and you shouldn't tolerate it. Get out of there and don't look back! You can read more about bullying in Chapter 4.

Involve an adult. If all else fails, tell an adult, like your parents or, if you're on school grounds, an administrator.

My Story

When I was in middle school, I was a "good kid." I did well in school, I was polite, I never got into any trouble. Eventually, I got tired of my "good kid" label and wanted to try out some bad behavior for a change. I tried shoplifting, for example, which is a really dumb, pointless, and quick way to ruin your life. I would have never gotten away with it if stores had the technology that they have today.

A few times, I encouraged my friends to do the same kinds of things I was doing. I didn't feel like I was bullying them into anything, but I definitely suggested that we do stuff like shoplift and smoke, and I was enthusiastic about it.

Now that I'm older, I realize why I wanted to involve my friends. Trying out bad behavior made me feel like a degenerate, criminal, loser freak… but I didn't want to be looked at that way. I thought that if I encouraged other kids to act on my level, I wouldn't be a freak. We would all be freaks, and that would make smoking (yuck) and stealing (yikes) okay. (News flash: They're not!)

Some of my friends joined me in those bad (and sometimes illegal) behaviors. But I distinctly remember one or two of my friends saying they didn't want to smoke or steal. They weren't interested, and furthermore, they didn't want to get in trouble with their parents. No matter how proud I was of all the stupid risks I was taking, they didn't budge.

At the time, I admired them for it. (And looking back now, I really admire them for it!) In fact, I remember being a little jealous of their resolve. I left them alone.

My habits may have seemed cool and dangerous at the time, but really, they were completely stupid and lame, and could have gotten me into serious trouble. Those friends who refused to join in had the right idea. I'm glad they stood up to me and said no!

How to Spot a Bad Friend

Nobody's perfect, and that includes your friends. However, there's a big difference between an imperfect friend and a bad friend. It's important to know the difference so that you can decide whether to keep the friendship alive... or to ditch the friendship entirely.

Here are some signs that you're dealing with a bad friend:

1. They bully you or others.

2. They're overly demanding of your time and energy.

3. They get mad at you constantly, despite your best efforts to be a good friend.

4. They pressure you into doing things you don't want to do.

5. The bad times in your friendship far outweigh the good.

6. You are constantly unhappy in the friendship.

7. You just know down deep inside that you've had it!

If you've tried absolutely everything and a friend is still making you miserable, it's time to cut him or her off. All friends fight every now and again, but if a friend is making you feel bad almost all the time and you're not getting much out of the friendship, you don't have to tolerate it. There are plenty of fish in the sea!

However, it's not always easy to speak up and end a friendship. In some ways, it's even harder than breaking up with someone (which you can read about on page 123). When a romantic relationship is over, it's over. But when you have to say farewell to a friendship, you risk a lot: losing other friends, having to change everything from your birthday invitee list to your seat in the cafeteria, upsetting people, and more. If Speaking Up were a subject in school, ending a friendship would be an advanced class!

If you've weighed your options and have decided to end a bad friendship, here's what to do:

Admit that you want out. Sometimes, the hardest thing to do is to admit that you're unhappy in a friendship. It's easy to get stuck in an endless cycle of trying to work on things and fix them… even when they're unfixable. But if your friend upsets or disappoints you time and time again no matter what you do, it's time to move on. Admit it to yourself so that you can take the next steps.

Hang out with different people. Think of the people who make you feel at ease and happy. Maybe they're not totally in the center of your world right now, but you know they're cool and fun to be around. Try hanging out with them for a while. Being happy and calm with other friends may help put your relationship with your toxic friend into perspective, and help you decide if you want to end it.

Try to exit peacefully. The end of a friendship doesn't have to be a big, dramatic confrontation. Sometimes, all you have to do is stop calling, stop getting together, and start hanging out with a new group of friends. The toxic friend may not even notice, depending on the situation.

But if not... If you know you can't end the friendship without talking to your friend first, here are some do's and don'ts for speaking up to a soon-to-be ex-friend.

Do: Be nice and calm.

You: I'm really sorry... but I have been really unhappy lately and I'd rather not hang out anymore. I hope you can understand.

Do: Accept the fact that he or she will have a reaction, and not necessarily a good one.

Friend: What are you talking about? This is coming out of nowhere! You're acting crazy! Why?

If this happens, don't use fighting words or cast blame. Remember, you're bringing up a pretty tough proposal that your friend might not expect: Of course your friend is going to react. To make this conversation go as smoothly as possible, keep your words brief and general. Avoid pointing fingers at the other person; try using "we" not "you." Remember, you're not fighting (those days are over) — you're separating.

Don't: Begin with accusations.

You: Because you've been a you-know-what to me for way too long and I'm sick and tired of it!

Do: Use reasonable "we" language.

You: As you know, we've been fighting a lot and we haven't been getting along. I'm really just ready to move on, and I think we'll both be happier this way in the long run. I'm sorry. (exit)

Even if your friend kicks and screams, she can never really dismantle the logic in this case. Eventually, the friend should realize that the friendship is over, and move on herself.

Here is another example, however, of how a friend might react to your friend breakup speech:

Friend: I'm really sorry — I swear I'll be better!

Do: Approach this response with caution.

Ask yourself if you been down this road before. If you've never spoken up to this particular friend before, maybe he or she deserves a second chance. But if you have tried this tactic already or you really don't see how things can change, maybe this friend has been given enough chances already.

At the end of the day, you choose your friends. Middle school friends should be fun and supportive. If they're not, speak up and change things.

My Story

It was like a scene right out of the movie *Mean Girls*. My friend and I were talking on the phone, making a plan to meet up and hang out. Usually, that meant that everyone on the planet also had to hang out so that nobody felt left out. This often ended up being a planning nightmare so this time I told my friend on the phone, "Let's keep it small."

Suddenly, I heard cackling on the other end of the phone. The friends I was suggesting we leave out of our gathering had been listening in on the entire conversation. They taunted me as if they had caught me in the act. I was so surprised and freaked out that I hung up the phone and cried hysterically. My mom asked what was wrong and I didn't want to tell her — I was so embarrassed by the interaction. I was sure I had done something terrible to those friends, and I didn't want my mom to see me so upset.

Now, looking back, I know that I did absolutely nothing wrong. They were being manipulative and a little ridiculous by tricking me. I wish I had said so at the time!

It wasn't until high school that I was able to say, "Hey, these friends suck. I'm making new ones." We didn't have much of a confrontation. These toxic friends didn't exactly fight to keep me around, and I simply stopped seeing them. I still had other friends, and I made new ones in different groups.

Once I got rid of those manipulative, unfair friends, I felt an enormous weight lifted off my shoulders. High school was a blast.

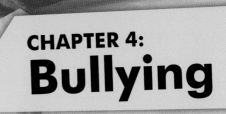

CHAPTER 4:
Bullying

Studies show that bullying reaches its peak in middle school, and it can be an extremely stressful experience for everyone involved. People remember childhood bullying for the rest of their lives, and if they don't speak up for themselves and others, they often live with regret in addition to trauma. Bullying only continues if other people let it happen. If nobody speaks up, the bullying won't stop.

Unfortunately, you can't erase bullying all by yourself. In fact, teachers and administrators have been trying to eliminate bullying for decades, and they still have a long way to go. However, you can do your part by identifying threatening behavior in your school and speaking up against it.

What is Bullying, Really?

People tend to throw the word around a lot as if it's a very simple idea. But if it were actually simple, then it would be a lot easier to eradicate.

In reality, bullying can range from playful teasing gone too far to physical violence. If somebody goes after you on Facebook about your clothes, it's not in-your-face or violent, but it is still a form of bullying. So how do you recognize bullying, as opposed to say, a fight with a friend?

Here are some telltale differences:

Signs of a Friend Fight:

1. An argument is only about the argument itself.

2. The actual fighting is restricted to the people involved.

3. Both people are still clearly friends, even if they're fighting.

4. The friends seem equal to each other. Neither friend has absolute power over the other.

5. The fight cools off eventually, and the friendship continues.

Signs of Bullying:

1. The fight includes mean-spirited teasing, pranks, or gossip. People feel cornered or exposed.

2. The fight includes a deliberately cruel silent treatment intended to punish someone.

3. One person or group is purposely trying to make someone else feel bad or humiliated.

4. One person or group is trying to force someone to do something he or she doesn't want to do.

5. The fight includes several people who were not involved in the original argument.

6. One person is being attacked by several people.

7. One person seems to hold all the power in the argument, while the other person has no say and no backup.

8. The fight includes racist, homophobic, or sexist slurs.

9. One person is actively trying to turn more people against the other.

10. Physical violence is involved.

11. The fight seems to have no possible end.

Here is an example of bullying that isn't loud or violent... but it definitely counts as bullying:

Christy: Carly had such an attitude the other day. I was about to freak out at her.
Erin: I know! She's just upset that she has greasy hair.
Christy: Oh my God... It's like a fountain of grease. Literally, a fountain.
Erin: We should email her from a fake account and advertise shampoo to her, because she needs to get the hint!
Christy: Oh my God, that is so funny. Yes! Let's do it!

No!!! Don't do it, Erin and Christy!

What Erin and Christy don't realize is that this type of email may actually traumatize Carly, possibly for the rest of her life. Even if these girls think it's just a funny, stupid thing to do one afternoon, bullying like this can cause serious damage. It can even result in the victim's suicide. In short, one tiny email can ruin many, many lives — including Erin's and Christy's. Both of them need to back off immediately.

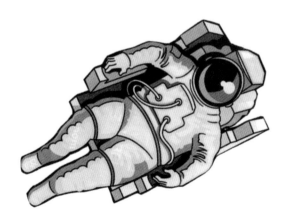

Here is another example of bullying using the "silent treatment," and by including others in the fight:

Jonica: Why are you so mad at me?
Kylie: (silence)
Jonica: Can't you at least talk to me?
Kylie: (silence)
Jonica: I'm really upset about this, come on!
Kylie: I'm not talking to you, and that's it.
　　(Enter Anna)
Anna: Hey, Jonica, what's up?
Jonica: Hey…
Kylie: Anna, I thought you were my friend. You're so two-faced.

We don't know why Kylie is so upset, but whatever the reason, she decided to retaliate by bullying Jonica. She is clearly using the silent treatment to punish Jonica and push her around, despite Jonica's best efforts to make amends. Then Kylie uses manipulative language to turn Anna against Jonica. Kylie is bullying both of them.

If Kylie doesn't want to talk to Jonica, that's fine, but she could have said it without the bullying and punishing. For example, she could have said, "I'm really upset about what happened, and I'm not quite ready to talk yet," and left it at that.

Here is another example of bullying. This time, the bully is using subtle language to get under somebody's skin, and the situation is unequal:

Brianna: So, Nico, welcome to the school.

Nico: Thanks.

Brianna: Do you want to come to a party this weekend?

Nico: Uhh… maybe…

Brianna: You're new here, you don't know anyone, and you're going to say no to a party that I'm inviting you to?

Nico: Uhh…

Brianna: Just kidding, there is no party. Can I eat your apple?

Nico: Okay…

Brianna: I hear you're good at math. I'm looking to copy someone's homework tonight. Is it cool if I borrow yours?

Nico: Uhh, I don't necessarily feel comfortable with that.

Brianna: Come on! Nobody will know about it. I swear. We're cool, right? I thought we were friends.

In this stomach-turning conversation, Brianna is clearly established in the school, while Nico is still finding her bearings. Brianna is definitely using her position to push this girl around. Apparently, Brianna's idea of welcoming Nico is to mess with her, embarrass her, say insincere things, and push her into things that make her feel uncomfortable. Brianna's not being outright mean, but she is still being a bully, even if all she's doing is confusing the heck out of Nico.

How to Handle Bullying

If you're being bullied or you see someone else being bullied, what do you do?

It's hard to think logically when bullying is happening. It can make you feel shocked, helpless, and angry. At its worst, bullying can silence you completely.

While there's no exact science to stopping a bully, there are many ways to speak up in a bullying situation and make sure that your voice is heard. And remember: If you can't stop the bully yourself, it's always okay (and a good idea!) to get an authority figure involved.

Here are some tips for dealing with bullying:

1. Remember: It's not your fault. Sometimes, victims of bullying believe that they deserve it, so they let the bullying happen without speaking up. The truth is, there is absolutely no excuse for bullying, ever. You hear all the time that bullies lash out because they really feel bad about themselves on the inside, and it's true. Most bullies have their own issues or they have been bullied themselves, so they're looking for a target and an audience on which to take their feelings out. It could be anyone.

2. Tell the person that he or she is being a bully. Believe it or not, people don't always realize that they're being a bully. Have you ever heard anybody say, "I'm going to be a bully now"? Probably not, because often people don't realize that what they're doing constitutes bullying! Telling them that they are acting like a bully may help stop them in their tracks.

3. Don't leave a friend high and dry. Stand up for a friend if he or she is being bullied. You would want the same thing done for you, right? Sit with your friend at lunch and, if a bully attacks, step up and say, "Leave my friend alone!" Sticking by your friend sends a message that you don't agree with the bully, and you're on your friend's side. Plus, it's harder to gang up on two people than one!

Of course, you should only do this if you feel safe. If you don't, you should go straight to an adult. (See #7)

4. Don't engage. Bullies want to upset people, and unfortunately, they often succeed. It's hard not to get upset when somebody is bullying you. However, if you don't play into a bully's games, he or she may eventually give up.

5. Never, ever support it. Bullies thrive on other people's encouragement. Even passively supporting bullying or laughing occasionally is enough to encourage the behavior. Bullies lose their power when they lose their support. Let them know that you don't believe in what they're doing and that you don't think it's okay.

6. Don't stoop to their level. You have a right to be mad at a bully, but that doesn't mean you should bully back. Tempting as it can be to take revenge on bullies, you don't want to stoop to their level and become a bully yourself. Let the real bully get in trouble here, and let living without the bullying be its own reward.

7. Get an adult involved. Telling an adult is crucial in a bullying situation. School officials, like teachers, guidance counselors, and security guards, should be trained to handle bullying situations big and small. If a bully isn't listening to you, an adult will! (For more on telling an adult, see page 86.)

8. Spread the word. The only way that bullying will disappear is if people keep talking about it. Share stories about bullying with your friends and family. Chat about it, read about it, and don't let the conversation die. (If you want to think even bigger about bullying, read more on page 94.)

9. Shoo the bullies out of your life. If your friends are constantly being bullies, it's time to find some new friends. This is one of the hardest, most painful changes to accept, but you can have a great time in school if you have positive, encouraging friends. What better way to speak up to bullies than by telling them you don't need them?

If you're seeking advice or help in a bullying situation, the Internet isn't always a good or reliable resource. Avoid anonymous chat or message forums. Leave it to the experts and people you trust. For reliable information on bullying, visit:

http://www.stopbullying.gov/what-you-can-do/teens/index.html
http://www.pacerkidsagainstbullying.org/
http://pbskids.org/itsmylife/friends/bullies/

For information on online bullying, head to:
https://www.facebook.com/safety/

Telling an Adult

Involving an adult can feel like a nuclear option reserved only for emergencies, and there's also peer pressure not to "tattle" on other people. On top of that, you might feel like an adult won't get the whole picture and could jump to the wrong conclusions about what's actually going on.

However, adults — like your parents, teachers, school administrators, or guidance counselors — have probably been through something similar in their lives, so they'll likely understand that you're feeling nervous about speaking up. Adults have real authority to do something about bullying, and even better, some adults are professionally trained to do something about it. At the very least, they can advise you on the next steps, and at best, they can make sure this kind of bullying never happens again.

Here are some tips on talking to adults about bullying:

Find out what your school has to offer. Your school should have a formal system for handling bullies. In some schools, for example, it's best to tell a guidance counselor or principal when bullying occurs. In other schools, simply talking to your teacher is enough to get the process started. Find out your school's process by asking a teacher or a guidance counselor. If nobody is responsive on the school level, your parents or another trusted adult might have to take the issue to the school superintendent or the board of education. It should be easy for kids to speak up about bullying to authority figures, but even if you have to talk to a few different adults, don't give up until someone listens to you.

Explain the situation thoroughly. You should give an adult as many details as possible, so do some prep before you speak with him or her. Answer as many of the following questions as you can. (If you can't answer many of these questions, speak up anyway and maybe the adult can help you find the answers.)

- *Can you name all or most of the bullying incidents?*

- *What happened, where, and when? Who was involved?*

- *What words were said?*

- *Were there any adults around? What did they do?*

- *How long has the bullying been going on?*

Also, if you have any evidence — like Facebook posts, emails, texts, or photos — bring it to the discussion!

You can request anonymity. If you're nervous about putting yourself front and center, you can try reporting the bullying anonymously. Tell your guidance counselor or teacher that you don't want your name mentioned if she intervenes. She should do everything she can to respect your request.

Asking for advice is okay. With some kinds of bullying, all you may need is advice, not an intervention. Ask a guidance counselor how you should handle the conflict. You might learn a lot! And if taking her advice doesn't produce results, she'll be familiar with the situation when you come back to her for more help.

Recognize When You Are the Bully

Even good people can be bullies sometimes. Did you know that a whopping 87 percent of middle school students switch their role from victim to bully at some point? An unfortunate cycle plays out: People who have been bullied become bullies themselves in order to feel like they have power. They may not recognize that they're doing the exact same thing that someone else has done to them, but bullying is bullying, no matter who does it or why. It is always wrong.

Here are some pro tips for confronting the bullying behavior in yourself and others:

Hit pause. If you or someone in your group is bullying someone else, hit the pause button. Mentally, step out of the group for a moment. Remember the signs of bullying from page 79. Are any of them happening right before your eyes? PAUSE!

Hit reverse. Time to call the situation off. Abort! De-escalate! Back off, and tell the other bullies to back off, too. If you're in a place where somebody is definitely going to get bullied, leave and get help. And bring as many of the would-be bullies with you as you can.

Switch gears. Do something else with all the energy that was going into bullying. Turn it into another conversation or a game. Run around. Do jumping jacks. Anything else! Soon, you won't even remember feeling the desire to push someone around.

Apologize. If you have bullied someone, saying you're sorry is a very brave, awesome thing to do. It won't erase the past, but it can make a really big difference both now and in the future. All too often, people wait until they're adults to apologize for bullying behavior, but you can help the victim heal sooner by apologizing right away.

Be a leader. It's not always easy to be a leader, but if bullying is going to stop, somebody has to step in and make the right decisions for the group. That person could very easily be you!

Remember, you don't have to actually do a mean deed to be a bully. By encouraging a bully (laughing along or saying nothing), you are also engaging in the bullying.

BULLYING QUIZ: Should you speak up?

1. Max and Aubrey have a disagreement, and they don't talk for a whole day. The next day, they get over it and continue being friends.

Bullying?   **Yes**   No

Why?

If yes, who should speak up, and how?

2. Anna makes a joke about Spencer's acne, and she knows he's sensitive about it.

Bullying?   **Yes**   No

Why?

If yes, who should speak up, and how?

3. Erika and Maria text Nicole from an unknown number, pretending to be Nicole's crush. They send Nicole sweet messages, and laugh at her when she buys it.

Bullying?   **Yes**   No

Why?

If yes, who should speak up, and how?

4. Ilana gets mad at Amani, so she tells everybody in school an embarrassing secret about Amani's family.

Bullying? **Yes** No

Why?

If yes, who should speak up, and how?

5. Lindsay pushes Jacquelyn to the ground when no one is looking.

Bullying? **Yes** No

Why?

If yes, who should speak up, and how?

6. Li Mei strongly disagrees with Maylin during a class discussion. She waits for Maylin to say her piece, then tells the class that she doesn't agree with her and why.

Bullying? **Yes** No

Why?

If yes, who should speak up, and how?

Answers:

1. No

Why?

Because Max and Aubrey seemed to resolve the problem quietly and fairly, and it stayed between them. They continued to be friends and the problem faded away.

2. Yes

Why?

Because Anna is making fun of Spencer to make him feel bad on purpose. This is bullying.

Who should speak up, and how?

Spencer should tell Anna that her words upset him. If she keeps making fun of him, he should tell an adult.

3. Yes

Why?

Because Erika and Maria made Nicole the victim of a mean prank that might humiliate her. This is bullying.

Who should speak up, and how?

Erika or Maria could have stopped the situation before it happened. One of them could have spoken up for Nicole, and suggested something else to do with their time. But since the texting has already happened, Nicole should tell an adult.

4. Yes

Why?

Because Ilana is trying to turn the school against Amani by humiliating her.

Who should speak up, and how?

Someone should tell Ilana to stop, whether it's Amani or a friend who hears the secret. Amani should also tell her parents, a guidance counselor, teacher, or administrator in her school, before the bullying escalates even further.

5. Yes

Why?

Because physical violence is always bullying.

Who should speak up, and how?

Jacquelyn should tell a school official, such as a guidance counselor or security guard. She should also tell her parents.

6. No

Why?

Li Mei might be passionate about politics, but that doesn't mean she's bullying Maylin. It's okay to disagree with someone, especially in a class discussion. She is not singling out Maylin; she is only expressing a contrary viewpoint on an issue. Good for her!

When the Bullies Aren't Classmates

So far, we've only talked about bullying between peers (other kids). But bullying can happen anywhere, and anyone can do it. The ways to speak up differ depending on the situation. Here are a few examples:

Sibling bullying isn't talked about very often, which is why it can be hard to speak up if you're experiencing it. If a relationship with a sibling resembles the behaviors on page 79, it is bullying. Period.

People often dismiss sibling bullying as simple rivalry, but there is a difference, and the damage done by sibling bullying can be profound. Bullying doesn't usually enter your home life, but you live with your sibling. If anywhere should be a "safe zone," it should be your home.

If speaking up to your sibling directly (using the tactics on page 83) isn't changing anything, talk to your parents or another adult. Tell them about individual incidents and about the overall relationship you have with your sibling. Hopefully, they will take the lead in steering your relationship right.

However, if your parents aren't helpful, you may be able to get advice from a school guidance counselor. They should direct you to some next steps, like counseling or mediation, or they may talk to your parents on your behalf.

We'll talk more about other kinds of family issues in Chapter 5 (page 96).

Adult bullies. Believe it or not, adults can be bullies too. Just like bullies your own age, adults can single people out and deliberately put them down. It's already inappropriate behavior for kids, but for an adult to behave that way is absolutely unacceptable.

If an adult in school crosses the line from authority figure to bully, you should tell your guidance counselor, parent, or principal immediately. The school is obligated to protect you and take appropriate action. Do not suffer in silence just because the bully is in a position of power. Bullying is always wrong.

TAKING IT FURTHER:
Spreading the Word on Bullying

Is bullying in your school a problem — and do you want to speak out in an even bigger way? You can spread the word using your student government, your creative energy, and that voice of yours!

Here are some ways to spread the word about bullying in your school and beyond:

Run for student government. Student government has the ability to enact change in your school and spread positive messages. You could run for student government and make anti-bullying one of your major political platforms. Or you can just speak to your class president about bullying and see what he or she can do.

Hang anti-bullying posters. Suggest that your student government hang anti-bullying posters around your school. Studies show that constant messages can actually make a difference. You just need permission from your school first.

Use the morning announcements. Whether it's your class president or your principal, somebody is probably delivering your morning announcements — and she might be open to suggestions. You can ask that she include anti-bullying messages every now and again — anything from "What is Bullying, Really?" quick facts (see page 78) to instructing students on where to go if they encounter bullying in the school.

Suggest a peer advocacy program. A peer advocacy program pairs student "advocates" with other students who may be targets of bullying, including students with disabilities. The advocate's job is usually to be a friend and watch out for potential bullying situations. You can encourage your student government, guidance counselor, or school principal to start a peer advocacy program and change some lives!

Be creative. Put on a play, start a discussion group, or launch a social media group filled with anti-bullying messages for your school. You'll be taking on a good cause and exercising your creativity at the same time!

CHAPTER 5:
Your Family

Speaking up within your family might be even more important than speaking up with your friends or crushes. Friends may come and go, but you live with your family, and you're attached to them for the rest of your life.

In this chapter, we'll talk about why it's worthwhile to speak up with your family, how to do it, and how to navigate any challenges. Remember, you're always going to be part of your family, and it's important that you feel heard and understood.

Why Now?

By your middle school years, you are starting to be a lot more independent from your family. You're making your own life choices, which is great! However, all of the intense emotional changes in middle school (see page 17) can lead to a confusing relationship with your family. Plus, as you get older, you may start to see your parents as true human beings: imperfect people who are different from you and have their own share of faults and problems. It can make for a rough transition.

During your middle school years, you may find yourself more likely than you were before to get upset with your parents. And your parents, for their part, may become more likely to get upset with you. Communication is the key to getting through this period smoothly, and yet sometimes all you want to do is slam the door in your mom's face.

It's not your fault that it's harder to communicate with your family right now — your body and mind are developing, your values are changing, and you're discovering who you really want to be... and that's normal. But if you don't speak up when you need help, when you don't feel appreciated, or even when you're happy or proud, your family won't know how or when to give you the support you need. You can help your family help you by telling them how you're feeling, what you're thinking, and what they can do about it.

Remember, other people in your family are going through their own changes and life stages, so they might not always be good at hearing you speak up (or speaking up for themselves).

Each family is different, and there are all kinds of dynamics at play within every family. Try out some of the techniques in this chapter and see what works best for you and your family.

When to Speak Up With Your Family

You don't need to speak up about absolutely everything. It's totally natural to want to be alone with your thoughts sometimes, especially if you've been dealing with an annoying sibling all day! So how do you know when to keep your thoughts to yourself?

Here are some scenarios in which speaking up with your family may help you:

• *When you disagree with them about something important (see page 103).*

• *When you need something that will make your life easier or better, such as a desk for doing homework, new curtains to help you sleep better, or a little privacy every now and again!*

- *When you are worried for a family member (for example, your sibling is starting to hang out with a dangerous crowd).*

- *When you are feeling particularly depressed, anxious, or stressed, and you need help (see page 108).*

- *When you need help with homework, studying for a test, or generally improving your grades.*

- *When you want to learn something new, like an instrument, or life skills like writing a check, and your family might be able to help.*

- *When you have been dealing with serious issues in school, like bullying, or issues with a friend or teacher (see page 108).*

- *When you are unhappy with how people in your family have been treating each other.*

- *When you are dealing with abuse or neglect at home, in which case you would probably inform someone outside of the family.*

- *When you are proud of yourself.*

- *When you are proud of another family member.*

- *When you just want to show some love.*

Know Your Role... Then Ditch It

A lot of people take on a role in their family. Some kids are the non-argumentative "good kids," others are "bad kids"; some play the protector of their siblings, others are the "shy" ones. There are endless kinds of roles to play within a family.

As you're growing up, you take cues from your family members and try to figure out your place in the family. Sometimes, your family may treat you a certain way — like the "bad kid," the "good kid," the "problem kid," the "black sheep," the "messy one," the "incapable one," the "smart one," the "athlete," the "kid with the future at Harvard." And the list goes on and on. Your family may constantly reinforce these labels, and you might take on the role because you believe that's what you're meant to do and who you really are. After all, your family knows you better than anyone else, right? Not always.

Roles help give people a context for the relationships in their family, and help people understand how they fit together. Roles are sometimes helpful: For example, your parents are the "responsible ones" and you can count on them to make sure you're fed, clothed, and taken care of. However, roles can be damaging and limiting, too. The "incapable" kid will always feel incapable, the "mediator" kid will always feel like he or she has to keep the peace, and the "bad kid" will always feel bad — even when they're all grown up and not living with their family anymore.

However, there's a big secret about family roles that you may not know: Roles are totally changeable, and in a way, they're completely false constructs. Everyone can be good at some things but bad at others. Anyone can be shy sometimes and outspoken other times. Anyone can be the silent mediator one minute but the aggressive agitator the next. Personalities aren't black and white.

If your role in your family is preventing you from speaking up for yourself, try rethinking who you are.

This isn't a quick or easy thing to do. Adults can spend years in therapy trying to undo the effects their childhood family role has had on them. You probably won't be able to change everything about your role right away, but change can start inside of you, and you can learn to speak up even if it isn't something that's expected of you.

In the beginning of this book, you learned that the best route toward speaking up is to question everything that might be holding you back, even things that seem unquestionable (page 23). Based on that idea, here are some questions to ask yourself about your family role:

- *What are some of the good things your family says about you?*

- *How about the negative things?*

- *If you have siblings, what do you think your role is compared to theirs?*

- *Is there anything you'd like to change about your role?*

- *Does your role allow you to speak up about the things you need or want, and does it ensure that your family will listen sympathetically?*

The first step to changing your role is to think about it critically. Over time, by thinking about it and bucking expectations (such as speaking up when no one expects it from you), you will probably be able to change it! Acting outside your role might throw some members of your family off at first, but keep in mind that your family loves you and wants you to feel safe, happy, and heard. Persevere, and they'll have to get on board eventually.

Remember, you're not stuck in a role if you don't want to be.

How to Speak Up to Your Family

You know your family better than anyone else. You know if your mom is temperamental, if your sibling is shy, if your dad is super understanding... whatever the combination of personalities may be. The trick is to work with the personalities you know so well, but also to defy the routine a little bit in order to speak up for yourself.

Here are some tips that might help you find that balance:

Never say never. You might think that your family will react a certain way if you speak up, but unless you try it, you'll never find out! It can feel scary and risky to make yourself heard, but if you stay silent you'll never know what you might have gained by voicing your opinion.

Step out of the argument. If you are in the middle of an argument with family, step away. People tend to be less understanding in the middle of a passionate fight. You can always offer your point of view later, once things have calmed down. It's much more likely that people will be willing to listen to you then.

Carve out some quality time. If you bring up something important during the morning rush, over text messages, or during a fight, you might not get the full attention you deserve. Make sure your family members are able to focus on you and what you have to say. If it's not going to happen right away, ask them to make some time later on.

Try to keep the conversation calm. If you keep calm, you can help steer the conversation away from becoming an argument. You'll be more likely to get your point across if you approach the situation calmly from the start rather than entering your chat with a combative attitude.

Be confident in your position. Be familiar with your point of view and stick to your stance. If it helps, you may want to run your points through your mind or write them down in advance so that you feel confident bringing them up later.

Be open to compromise. Sometimes, a family member may bring some good ideas to the table, too. Hear them out and respect their point of view. Maybe you can reach some sort of a compromise. (See page 61 for more information on compromising.)

Be patient. Don't get discouraged if everything doesn't work out the first time you speak up with a family member. Remember, your speaking up may be new for them, so they might need some time to process what's going on.

Feel proud. You take a risk by speaking up. You're putting yourself out there, but people may still disagree with you. Whether it's your family, friends, crushes… whomever, the point remains: Just because somebody disagrees with you, that doesn't mean you're wrong. You can leave the conversation with your head held high knowing that you stood up for what you believe in.

The following three conversations take place between Kate and her dad. In this hypothetical family, every kid plays soccer. That's just the way it is, and just the way it always has been. Now that she's in middle school, Kate realizes that she isn't enjoying soccer at all. It's a confusing realization because she's been told her entire life that soccer is really important, and for the longest time, she believed it. But is it true? Not to Kate, at least not anymore!

Which conversation is the best way for Kate to handle this?

Conversation A

Kate: Hey, Dad, I wanted to ask you something.

Dad: Sure, go ahead.

Kate: Why do you want me to play soccer?

Dad: Well, you're good at it, and you always liked it.

Kate: Yeah. I guess so.

Dad: Why do you ask?

Kate: Oh, no reason. I was just asking.

Dad: Okay then. Ready for dinner?

Kate: Yep. I'll just go wash my hands.

Conversation B

Kate: Can I ask you a question?

Dad: Sure.

Kate: Why do I have to play soccer? I hate it and you're forcing me to do it, and it sucks!

Dad: Hang on there. You play soccer because you're good at it and you've always liked it.

Kate: No, I don't! I suck at it and you're being a bad parent by making me do it.

Dad: Don't speak to me that way.

Kate: Well, you never listen to me!

Dad: Enough. Go to your room.

Conversation C

Kate: Can I ask you a question?

Dad: Sure.

Kate: How would you feel if I told you that I'm not into soccer anymore?

Dad: What? You're not?

Kate: It just feels like you really want me to play soccer, but I've been thinking about it a lot lately… and I'm really not that into it anymore.

Dad: What changed? You've always liked soccer!

Kate: I just think I want to try other things. I'm not having fun playing soccer like I used to.

Dad: I'm surprised. Do you have to quit this second? Championships are next week.

Kate: How about I play in the championships and then quit?

Dad: Hmm… How about you play in the championship and then we'll talk about it?

Kate: Okay. I'm going to hold you to it!

Dad: All right.

Conversation A: No! In this conversation, Kate backed down almost immediately. She started to speak up for herself, but in the end, she couldn't go through with it. Maybe she thought her dad would get angry or that he would be able to read her mind. Unfortunately, because she didn't speak up about what she really wanted, nothing changed.

Conversation B: No! In this conversation, Kate did speak up for herself, but she came out swinging and looking for a fight. She is obviously very passionate about the issue, which is understandable. However, she acted on those feelings in a way that probably won't get her what she wants, and she was disrespectful toward her dad in the process. No wonder Dad didn't take it well.

Conversation C: Yes! In this conversation, Kate hasn't gotten what she wanted yet, but she probably stands a much better chance of getting it than if she had gone with conversations A or B. Why? She respected her father's feelings on the issue, she approached it calmly, and she didn't back down! She even struck a compromise: She'll play in the championships, but afterward they'll talk again about her quitting soccer. Who knows — maybe he'll warm up to the idea by the time they discuss it. Or maybe playing in the championships will remind Kate of what she loves about playing soccer. Whatever happens, Kate will know that she spoke up for herself and her dad heard her.

Speaking Up About the Really Tough Stuff

It's one thing to speak up to your family about playing soccer next season... it's quite another to speak up about something really serious, like depression, drugs, major difficulties in school, identity and sexuality (see page 118), or abuse. During difficult and very complicated times, it's more important than ever to speak up to your family, but it can be really scary. What if they don't understand? What if they overreact? What if... what if?

Your family should be able to help you through difficult times more than anyone else can. They are responsible for your well-being, and they're also responsible for helping you through life's rough patches and making you stronger. Most members of your family have been through difficult times, too, so they should know what steps to take — or be able to help you find the right resources if they don't. Hopefully, you can trust them to take care of you, protect you, and take the next steps to help you feel safe and happy. If they don't know what's going on with you, then they can't help you get the support you need.

Here are some tips to getting past that hump and speaking up to your family in difficult situations:

Don't worry if you are confused. It's very hard to speak up about things that you don't fully understand yourself, but telling your parents or another family member that you don't fully understand something is speaking up. Saying, "I don't know what's going on but I just feel sad sometimes," or "I'm just not doing well in school but I don't know why," or "I don't know what I need, but I get a bad feeling about this new girl I've been hanging out with" is a start, and hopefully your family member can help you figure out what's happening. All of these confusing feelings are part of the human experience, and it's okay to express them.

Put the information out there. Again, parents aren't mind readers. They will only be able to go on what you give them. If you act sad or depressed or angry, they may notice, but they won't know exactly what's up. They might think you need space or advice when what you really need is for them just to listen. Give them as much information as you can — even if it feels awkward to say it out loud — so that they can help you in the best way possible.

Help your family help you. If your family's approach isn't working, try telling them to use another route. Maybe they're looking at the situation too harshly or judgmentally — or maybe they're not dealing with it at all. For example, if they're saying, "Never hang out with that girl again!" instead of what you need (which may be more along the lines of, "I should talk to your friend's parents about getting her some help"), it may help to let them know that you're looking for a different approach. Also, if something is working, you could tell them to keep it up (see "My Story" on page 112).

Speak up immediately if somebody is hurting you. Whether it's a teacher, sibling, classmate, friend, or boyfriend or girlfriend, if someone is bullying, abusing, or acting inappropriately toward you, tell your parents or another trusted adult. Try to remember as many details as possible, along with dates and places, if you know them.

A No-Speak-Up Family

Some families are just never, ever going to respond the way you want them to. Unfortunately, some families don't take emotions seriously or they don't know how to handle emotions at all. The unfortunate rule of speaking up is this: You can change the way you act, but you can't change other people entirely.

If you feel like your family will never let you speak up no matter what you do, you can reach out to your school guidance counselor, who may be able to help you and your family navigate your relationship. She might recommend a therapist or social worker, or be able to talk with you herself.

If you can't speak up in your family, keep connections strong with other trusted friends, adults, mentors, and people who offer you a different perspective. Remember, not all adults want to suppress your voice, even if your family isn't especially responsive. Speaking up is very important, and it's worth fighting for.

The Good Stuff

Sure, there are plenty of reasons to speak up in your family when things are rough… but what about when they're going well?

Maybe you were proud of something you did (a good grade, a nice save in soccer, or an excellent night of babysitting your siblings), but you didn't get the recognition you wanted. That's a great reason to speak up. Everybody wants to be recognized and appreciated, and there is absolutely no shame in asking!

Here are some examples of speaking up in order to share something you're proud of:

Jada: Hey, look at the A I got on the algebra test. Wanna hang it on the fridge?

Maddy: So, I took care of the baby for three hours last night, and he didn't cry once! Can a girl get a thank you? Or… some extra TV time tonight would be nice!

Jackie: Check it out — I made something in *Minecraft* for the first time. What do you think?

Shruti: I spoke up for myself! Did you notice?

What if you want to tell a family member that you love her or that you're grateful to have her? This kind of interaction can often be a bit uncomfortable, especially if you don't come from an affectionate family. Saying it out loud, though, can help strengthen your family relationships, and you may even introduce some affection into an affection-free family.

Jada: I know I'm not always nice to you, but I love you very much.

Maddy: You're the best sister on the face of the earth.

Jackie: It would be great if we went on a trip just you and me, Mom, don't you think?

Shruti: Can we start hugging when we say hello to each other? My friend's family does that, and I think I would like it a lot.

My Story

When I was younger, I was obsessed with food: how to avoid it, how many calories were in each little thing I ate, how much I would have to exercise to burn off a carrot (a carrot!!).

I didn't say anything to my parents about my eating disorder, ever. They saw the evidence on my body and in my behavior toward food, but when they tried to talk to me, I shut them out. I was embarrassed and I didn't know what to say.

I remember one Thanksgiving, I ate a really big meal. I felt like I had to, because Thanksgiving is a pretty food-centric holiday and I felt like I was being watched. Afterward, I retreated to the living room and watched TV silently. I felt awful. Physically and emotionally, I wasn't used to eating so much. I felt sick, like I had put on 100 pounds (I hadn't, of course; I was still skin and bones). I also felt so sad, and I couldn't put it into words.

My father asked me, "How do you feel after eating like that? Do you feel depressed?" I said, "Yes," and then I withdrew from the conversation. That was it.

It was such a small thing, but on that day he used a very different approach from what people (family, school nurses, teachers, friends) had previously taken with me. He was being empathetic and curious, not terrified or confused. He was asking me my perspective, rather than reflecting how the world saw me. It was different from saying, "You're too skinny," "Eat this right now!" and "Why are you so worried about your weight? You're beautiful the way you are," which I had heard before from other people.

To this day, I still remember that simple question my dad asked me.

Looking back, I wish I had told my family what I needed. I knew deep down that I wanted my parents to keep trying to talk to me, even though my behavior was showing them that I wanted to be left alone. I wish, on that day, I had replied to my father, "Yes. That meal made me depressed. Help me. Don't be afraid to help me. Help me understand. Keep asking me questions. Don't give up."

Knowing myself, I don't think I would have been able to open up to my dad like that in middle school. My emotions were big and confusing and I don't think I — or most other middle school kids — would have been able to be emotionally open like that. But it might have made a huge difference if I'd voiced my feelings that day — even if it was hard to do so.

It took many years to recover completely from my eating disorder, but regular therapy and growth eventually cured me. Speaking up effectively is still a day-to-day battle, however, and one that I'll never stop fighting!

CHAPTER 6:
Crushes and Relationships

During your middle school years, crushes and relationships start to play a major role in the lives of you and your friends. They're not required, of course. You can actually go your entire middle school life without having a crush or a relationship and turn out just fine. But for some, they are very important, and for others, they are practically obsessions!

It's Not Easy

Speaking up in relationships is not only about telling somebody you like him or her or asking that person out. Sure, that is part of it. But there are other points in a relationship when speaking up is just as important. In this chapter, we'll talk about speaking up at every stage of a crush or relationship — at the beginning, in the middle of it, and at the end. Learning to understand your feelings and speak up with a crush or in a relationship can really help everyone involved.

Asking Someone Out

If you are totally sure that you are into somebody and you want to ask the person out, go for it! There are tons of ways to go about it: by email, in person, by text, in a handwritten note, via carrier pigeon… the message remains the same. But many people feel nervous — or even scared — about asking someone out.

Here are a few things that might be in your way — and ways to combat them:

Fear of rejection. This is classic — even adults feel it! As with any other form of speaking up, you are taking a risk when you ask someone out. No matter how many signs or signals your crush is sending you, you can't predict if he or she will want to go out with you or not. One thing is for certain, though: You won't know until you ask the question. Get as much information as you can about how your crush feels about you and take the plunge! If he or she says no, it'll be awkward and difficult for a little while, but eventually you'll move on.

Isn't this supposed to happen in a particular way? Maybe you heard that a boy is supposed to ask a girl out and not the other way around. Or that you can only go out with someone of a certain social standing. Or that you have to do it in person and not via, say, a note. These are all just myths. There is no right way to ask someone out, period! If you're going to do it, do it in a way that makes you feel comfortable.

What does it mean once we're "going out"? Excellent question… and honestly, it's not always clear in middle school. Relationships are just starting to happen in earnest during the preteen years, and for one couple it can mean one thing, and for another couple, it can mean something completely different. Speaking up about your expectations for a relationship is really important in middle school because almost everyone has a different idea of what a relationship should look like.

Like an addition equation, a relationship is only the sum of its parts. That's it. You contribute stuff to the relationship, and your partner contributes other things. There is no mysterious lightning bolt that suddenly grants you different privileges, a new life, a new look, or a new brain once you are in a relationship. It is exactly what you and your partner make it!

You have to be proactive to get what you want out of a relationship. For example, you don't suddenly go to the movies every weekend with your partner because you're in a relationship. One or both of you have to suggest it and make it happen. To take another example, you shouldn't expect to hear "I love you I love you I love you" automatically just because you're in a relationship. People have different definitions of love and different reasons for saying "I love you."

Maybe it's just a crush. This is a great reason not to ask someone out. If you're not ready to be in a relationship, don't worry about it! You don't need to act on every little crush. In fact, a crush can be fun on its own: no complications, no risks, just the thrill. Enjoy it, and don't stress over taking it to another level.

Rejecting Someone.

If somebody asks you out and you're just not into it, don't be afraid to reject the person. You don't want to get caught up in a relationship with someone you don't really like. Just remember: Be kind. You can really hurt someone if you reject him or her in a mean way. "I'm sorry, I really like you but I'm not really interested in a relationship" is much nicer than "Um, seriously? You and me? Never!"

If the person won't take no for an answer and continues to bother you, tell an adult.

Questioning Your Identity

Maybe you're not interested in the "girlfriend" and "boyfriend" formula that dominates your school. Luckily, "boyfriend + girlfriend = relationship" isn't the only formula that exists.

Kids who are gay, bisexual, transgender, asexual, or questioning face many challenges during their middle school years. These range from identifying their sexual orientation to being bullied, and eventually being comfortable in their own skin (see page 108 for more about speaking up in your family). For now, you may be dealing with unknowns, like: What if I'm not like everyone else? What if I'm tired of girls only wanting to be my friend? What if I don't like boys? What if I feel like I'm not comfortable in my body? What does it mean? Does it even mean anything?

Figuring out who you are in middle school is difficult for most kids. If you feel different from your friends or classmates, or worse, persecuted by them, it's even harder. The statistics are tragic: Gay youth are four times more likely to take their own lives than straight kids, and a quarter of transgender kids make suicide attempts at some point.

However, if you feel like you don't necessarily fit the mold in your school or town, you're not alone. Even if you don't feel ready to "come out" in a formal sense, you can speak up for yourself by reaching out to supportive people or finding a group that can guide you through this difficult period.

If you feel comfortable, look for support from the standard outlets: friends, family, and school guidance counselors. However, if you'd rather look elsewhere, check out some of these resources:

- **The It Gets Better Project** (http://www.itgetsbetter.org/) curates tales of inspiration about people who have been through it all — and have come out on top.

- **The Human Rights Campaign** (http://www.hrc.org/resources/category/coming-out) provides guidance and resources on coming out.

- **The Trevor Project** (http://www.thetrevorproject.org/) provides crisis intervention and suicide prevention for lesbian, gay, transgender, and questioning youth. You can call their 24 hour hotline at 1-866-488-7386.

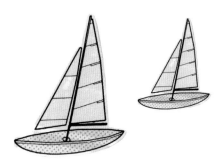

Drawing Boundaries

Drawing boundaries is really important and can be one of the most challenging parts about speaking up in a relationship. Drawing a boundary means that you're telling your partner what you're comfortable with and what you aren't. You are letting that person know when he or she has crossed the line, or at the very least, where your lines are. If you aren't clear about what your boundaries are, your partner won't know how to respect them. Remember, nobody can read your mind.

Here's an imagined set of personal boundaries:

• *I can't receive phone calls or texts after a certain time, or my parents will be mad.*

• *I'm not ready to go further than kissing right now.*

• *I don't want to spend so much time with your friends.*

• *I feel like we hang out all the time, and sometimes I need space.*

• *I don't like it when you smoke around me.*

Other boundaries may look a little more like needs:

• *I need you to be honest with me no matter what.*

• *I need you to pay more attention to me.*

- *I need you to tell me how you feel.*

- *I need us to start doing stuff outside of school.*

When you draw your boundaries, be firm. Don't worry what your partner will think: You're in the driver's seat just as much as your partner is. Sure, you could try to strike a compromise if it seems appropriate (see page 61 for tips on compromising), but if an issue is really important to you, don't back down. This is your relationship too, and you have the right to make it as comfortable and awesome as possible.

Here are some more tips on dealing with boundaries in relationships:

Trust your gut. Your instincts are usually right on! If something makes you feel weird or uncomfortable, even if you can't quite put your finger on why, it probably shouldn't be happening. Your gut usually steers you right, so be sure to listen to it. That's also just good life advice!

Expect some uncertainty. If you're not entirely sure where your boundaries lie, that's okay. Feeling uncertain is normal! You shouldn't put pressure on yourself to have all the answers right away. Saying "I'm not sure how I feel about that" also counts as speaking up. Maybe you just need some time to yourself to think things through or you need to try a few different boundaries before you find the right ones for you.

Don't tolerate a jerk. If you draw your boundaries and your partner repeatedly doesn't listen to you or tries to talk you out of your own feelings (as if that's even possible!), it's time to leave him or her in the dust. Life is too short to be spent hanging out with jerks! See page 123 for tips on breaking up, and page 125 for information about potentially abusive relationships.

Making Things More Fun

A relationship shouldn't be all about boundaries and rules. Sure, relationships are work, but they should be mostly fun. Otherwise, what's the point?

Maybe you're bored in your relationship and need a little something more. Or maybe you really care about your partner and you haven't expressed it yet. Speaking up can help!

Here are some ways to give your relationship a little bit of a boost:

Suggest something new. Bring a new idea to the table. Try saying, "Let's go for a walk!" or "Let's talk about your family, I know nothing about them!" or "Let's play catch!" Sometimes, new things — particularly fun new things — are just what a couple needs.

Give the person a present for no reason. Nothing says "you're great" better than a little gift — not for the person's birthday or for a holiday, but for no reason at all. (It's even better that way!) You don't have to get anything expensive; in fact, you can make them something, write them something, or take them to a special place that means a lot to you. It's a sweet thing to do and an easy way to show the person how you feel. At the very least, it's an opportunity to show off your crafting, writing, singing, or artistic skills!

Open up! Saying "I'm having fun!" or "I really like you" every now and again is a great way to keep a good relationship going. Even if it feels like you're stating the obvious, saying it out loud makes your experience more real for you and your partner!

Breaking Up

Unfortunately, even great relationships don't always last forever. Maybe you're bored or unhappy, or you're interested in something (or someone) new. Whatever the reason, the relationship is cooked. It's time to break up!

Breaking up is never easy, and it takes an effort on your part to speak up. You have to initiate a really difficult chat, and at the end of it, you have no idea how your partner will react. Maybe the person will feel hurt, angry, or completely surprised. Unless it's a totally mutual decision (which does happen sometimes), a breakup usually sucks for everyone involved. At least for a little while.

The good news about breakups is that while they're painful and annoying, they are usually pretty quick. Once you've made up your mind that you want to get out of the relationship, you're only a conversation away from being broken up. You're not working things out — you're ending them and going your separate ways. After all, what takes more work: a quick, difficult, uncomfortable breakup, or a relationship you don't want to be in that drags on and on?

Here are some tips on speaking up and breaking up:

Do it one-on-one. However you break up with someone (by note, text, in person, whatever), make sure that your partner receives the message alone. Don't do it in front of the person's friends. The embarrassment might add insult to injury.

Keep your message brief and firm. You don't have to go into a long list of what went wrong in the relationship. If you do that, you might invite an argument or counterpoint. This is a breakup, not a discussion. If it helps, write down your main points and go over them a few times before you talk to your partner.

Be kind. It's important to be kind during a breakup. You want this conversation to go as smoothly as possible. You don't want to hurt anyone, and you definitely don't want to engage in a battle of mean words.

Expect a reaction. People react when you break up with them: That's the nature of a breakup! Don't be surprised if the other person is sad, a little angry, or a little confused. It's natural for the person to have strong feelings, but don't let his or her reaction sway you from your position.

Give it space. Sometimes a breakup needs space and time to heal. After the breakup, try not to engage with your ex for a while. Eventually, the dust should settle and both of you will move on, and maybe even be friends.

Which breakup line is the best?

A. "Can we talk? I'm just really bored with everything and don't wanna go out anymore. Oh no, you're not gonna cry, are you?"

B. "Can we talk? I really like you a lot and we've had fun together, but I just want to move on. I'm so, so sorry. I'll be around if you need to talk, but I think we should just give each other space for a bit."

C. "So, remember that time you told Nick about my private family life? And how about that time you forgot to call me when you said you would? And remember when you made fun of my shoes? I'm just really not happy about those things, and I want to break up."

The answer is: B!

A is far too careless, and she made fun of her partner's natural reaction.

C is way too long-winded, and it invites an argument. (Wouldn't you argue back if someone accused you of stuff like that?)

B is short, gentle, and final.

Abusive Relationships

When you hear the word "abuse," your first thought might be of physical violence. Yes, a violent partner is certainly abusive, and you should tell an adult immediately if someone is physically abusing you.

However, there are many, many other signs of an abusive relationship that can be a bit more subtle than actual physical violence. If you recognize them early, you can speak up for yourself and break up before any serious damage is done.

Here are some signs of abuse in a relationship:

• *Your partner is constantly trying to keep tabs on you in a controlling way. He keeps asking for status updates and demands answers on every little thing.*

• *You feel like you are losing control of the situation, and it's a huge distraction from the rest of your life.*

• *Your partner makes you feel like everything is your fault, even the things that he or she clearly did wrong.*

• *Your partner acts like a bully toward you (see page 79 for signs of bullying).*

If these are traits of your relationship, you should break up now and distance yourself from that person. If your ex-partner won't let you leave the relationship (even if it's through the "I'm so sorry" dance), that's also a sign of abuse. Don't be ashamed — this kind of thing happens more often than you think. Tell a parent or a guidance counselor. An adult should be able to protect you and make sure you have the space you need to keep from your ex.

CHAPTER 7:
School Life

So far, we've covered speaking up in situations with friends, family, crushes, and bullies. In this chapter, we'll go into more detail on how to take what you've already learned about speaking up and apply it to real-life scenarios — at school, during sports activities, or when you are volunteering.

In the same way that you speak up with your friends, family, and crushes, speaking up in school means pushing through your fear and taking risks. If you've already developed self-confidence by speaking up with your family and friends, it'll be easier for you to speak up in situations where roles — like teacher-student, director-actor, and coach-player — are more rigidly defined. Speaking up is about asserting who you are, expressing yourself when things aren't going the way you want them to, and sometimes even being a leader.

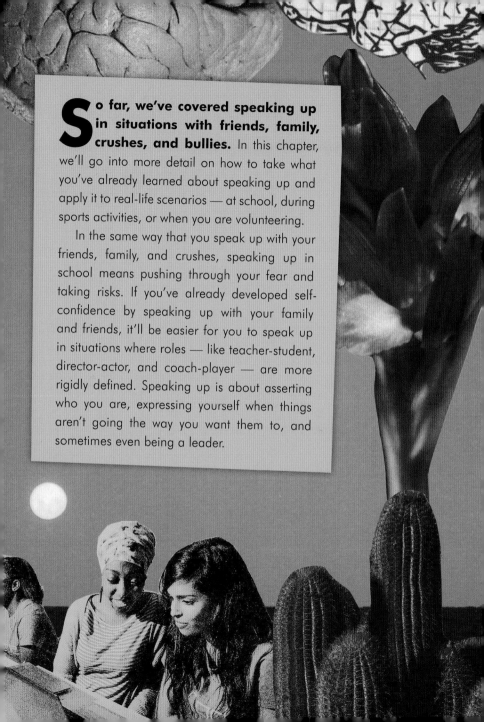

Reasons to Speak Up in School

There are tons of reasons to speak up in school. Here are some of the big ones:

- *You have something to add to a class discussion or group project.*

- *You want to lead a school discussion or group project.*

- *Participation in a discussion or activity is against your religious or personal beliefs, or a health or emotional issue is barring you from participating in a discussion or activity.*

- *A subject is difficult for you, and you need help.*

- *A teacher wasn't clear about the instructions for an assignment or test.*

- *A discussion or statement offends you.*

- *You witness discrimination within the school system, such as a teacher only calling on boys.*

- *A teacher or administrator behaves inappropriately or crosses the line into bullying or abuse (see page 94).*

- *You want to help improve things in your school, in areas such as bathroom cleanliness, food options, or field trips.*

- *You believe you deserved a better grade than the one you got.*

- *A teacher or administrator is unfairly singling you out or ignoring you.*

The Everyday Stuff

Speaking up in school doesn't just have to happen around major issues or events. You can practice speaking up every day in class, in the halls, and in the cafeteria. In addition to the speaking up tips you've learned in previous chapters, here are some school-specific speaking up tips:

Raise your hand and keep it up. Your contribution is important in every class discussion. If you have something to add, raise your hand! What's the worst that can happen? You get a question wrong? Somebody disagrees with you? Either way, you'll learn something new, and your voice will be heard.

Ask for help. If you need help with a subject, don't be embarrassed to ask questions either in class or after class. Everyone needs extra help from time to time. You don't want to fall behind because you were too embarrassed to ask for it.

Don't be afraid to disagree. If you disagree with a classmate who has been vocal about his or her opinion, don't be afraid to voice your disagreement in a class discussion. In fact, sometimes the class can benefit from a little debate. Your opinion is valid, so don't simply cave in to someone else's way of thinking if you disagree. Remember, if an argument breaks out, you can always agree to disagree!

Speak up about your needs. Teachers can't read your mind. If you are unable to do something in school because of an injury, illness, disability, or if you just get anxiety, tell your teacher, guidance counselor, or parents. The school should be willing to accommodate you if you've encountered a real obstacle.

Lead group projects. Don't be afraid to take the lead. You are just as capable of taking charge as anyone else in your class. Remember the confidence tips from page 48: Fake it until you make it, don't apologize, and work through your fear! If you feel like you'd make the best leader in a group project, go for it! Go over the assignment, facilitate an awesome, productive discussion with your group (a good leader is open to ideas), and delegate responsibilities.

Defy the boys vs. girls statistics a little each day. Even though girls tend to perform better than boys in school, studies show that they're quieter when it comes to class discussions and group projects. They apologize more, they raise their hands less, and they shy away from leading.

This isn't because boys are better. Boys don't hold some secret knowledge that girls aren't aware of. A lot of these patterns develop because of subtle discrimination: Girls get the message that they're supposed to be quiet, while boys can be as unruly as they please and still be heard in the classroom. Teachers may tend to call on boys more and listen to boys' responses more thoughtfully than they would listen to those of girls.

This type of discrimination isn't right, but sometimes it's difficult to spot. However, you can help change the statistics a little each day by staying confident, speaking up, and taking leadership roles. Show the world that you are not going to be ground down into another statistic and that your voice is worth hearing.

The Big Stuff

Beyond classroom discussions and homework help, there are many reasons to speak up about larger issues in your school. Sometimes, it may feel like you don't have much of a voice when it comes to these important issues. Teachers and administrators are in charge, and you are just the powerless student, right?

Well, yes, they are in charge, and you have to listen to them and follow the rules. But if you think about it, your school was made to serve you. You are entitled to get the best, fairest education possible. Therefore, you have every right to voice your opinion when it comes to significant decisions and policies. You're not supposed to run in the halls or chew gum, but there's no rule about expressing your opinion to the school authorities.

Here are some tips for speaking up about larger school issues:

Call out your teacher. If a teacher acts unfairly (if he or she gives you a grade you don't feel you deserve), talk to him or her after class. Address the issue calmly, privately, and try to avoid an accusatory tone. Frame the conversation as a discussion rather than a fight. For example, "I was hoping to find out why you gave me this grade and to point out few things you may have missed" is better than "How could you give me this grade?! I did everything you asked!" At the very least, you'll get a better explanation of why you got the grade you did, and at best, he or she might actually change your grade.

Call out your administrators. Your teacher isn't the highest-level authority you can report to. If your teachers aren't responding when you speak up, or if you have an issue that applies school-wide (like unhealthy cafeteria food or discrimination problems), you can talk to your principal. For added support, you should talk to your parents and guidance counselor first. Maybe they'll back you up with a letter or a call to the administrators.

Run for student government. If you want to make real change in your school, you can run for student government. Of course, there is a limit to what you can do in your role as class president or treasurer, but being in student office puts you one step closer to the administration and makes it easier for you to point out issues like bullying, discrimination, school sanitation, cafeteria food quality, activity costs, field trip destinations, and more!

Report abuse or inappropriate behavior. Any abuse, inappropriate behavior, or bullying by teachers or administrators should be reported immediately. Tell your parents or another trusted adult, and they should report the behavior to the principal or superintendent of the school. An adult should know whether or not something illegal has taken place, and if so, he or she should also contact the police. (Check out this website for more specific information: https://www.childwelfare.gov/pubs/usermanuals/educator/educatord.cfm.)

Speaking Up About Extracurricular Activities

You probably have some extracurricular activities on your schedule: piano lessons, soccer, theater, horseback riding, volunteer work, debate team… whatever you're into! Staying busy is great, but since these are extracurricular activities (aka optional, unlike school), you should feel even more entitled to speak your mind. You are there to have fun, play fair, get a chance to learn new skills, and maybe be a part of a community. If you have something to say about your extracurricular activity, speak up!

Here are some activity-specific tips on speaking up:

Go after the activities you want. In an ideal world, which activities (that exist in your school or community) would you really, really want to do? Talk to your parents, and try to work something out so you can do them (see page 103 for more on speaking up in your family). Even if it seems far-fetched to you (scuba diving in the ocean), your parents might be able to find a way to make it work (scuba diving lessons at the local pool).

Speak up against unfairness. Just like you would talk to your teacher if you thought he or she was being unfair, talk to your coach, instructor, administrator, or whoever is in charge of your activity if you smell injustice. For example, if your softball coach tells you to bunt every single time and won't let you hit, that's not fair at all. Don't just assume that you're not good enough to hit: Talk to the coach, find out what's up, and tell him you want to hit in the future (see Janelle's example on page 14).

Ask for help. As we've mentioned before, there's a lot happening in your body and mind in middle school. Your brain and body are changing, so things that seemed easy last year might be frustrating this year. For example, learning a language or perfecting your jump shot might take more effort than ever before. Again, don't just assume that you're "bad at something" when the truth is your body and mind are just adjusting. Ask for help. Talk to the instructor or coach.

Show off your talents. In some cases, your talents might be overlooked among other people's talents. For example, in a big theater group, maybe you haven't had the chance to show the teacher your amazing singing skills. You don't always have to wait around for an opportunity. At some point you can tell your teacher that you are a great singer and that you would like to show them when he or she has the time to listen. This would demonstrate a lot of bravery... which is crucial for the stage!

Quitting. If you're just not interested in an activity or it's making you miserable, quitting is an option. They say "nobody likes a quitter," but nobody likes a grumpy person who does things that make her unhappy, either! If you want to quit an activity, talk to your parents, coach, or advisor about it (see page 105 for more on how to quit).

My Story

Back in 7th grade I went through a slightly chubby phase. When I go through old pictures, I realize I looked just fine — but at the time, I couldn't accept how I looked, and I was very sensitive about it.

One day, our school nurse paid a surprise visit to our gym class. She ordered us to line up in a single file, with boys and girls in the same line. She set up a weight scale at the front of the line and demanded that we each step on the scale one by one. The worst part? She actually called our weights OUT LOUD, and a classmate of mine was ordered to take down the numbers on a sheet of paper.

My friends and I (even the slim ones!) ran into the locker room to hide, but we were eventually discovered and forced to step onto the dreaded scale. When it came to my turn, I wasn't exactly subtle about my anguish. I believe I stomped onto the scale and sighed loudly. The nurse yelled at me for my attitude. What else could I do? I obeyed. She weighed me, my classmate took down my number, and I went back to gym class, beyond traumatized.

When I got home, I broke down. I was mortified by my weight, and there it was, being put on display for the world to see at the hands of an authority figure. I told my mother about what had happened, and she told me I was right to be angry with the nurse. She suggested that she call the principal and complain, and I hesitantly agreed. While it was great to have her on my side, I was worried I would get into trouble with the principal and that my humiliation would only deepen.

The next day, the principal called me into her office. My initial anger had sort of worn off by then, so I was deeply embarrassed and nervous to be the center of so much attention from the most influential person in the school. (It still involved my weight, after all!) Instead of meeting me inside her office, the principal met me in the hallway and took a walk with me around the school. It was weird and different. I went to a big public school, so getting personal attention from the principal herself made me feel strange and bashful, but kind of important too. This stately, intimidating woman was treating me with respect — like we were just two equals taking a walk.

As it turned out, the principal had no idea the nurse had lined everyone up like that, and she was angry about it, too. She also shared a story with me about her childhood: Apparently when she was my age, the school had all the girls line up to have their uniform measurements taken in front of the whole school! She said it was a very humiliating experience, and she sympathized with me greatly. She apologized to me: the principal of my school. The most powerful person in my little world. Apologizing to me?

Then, she did something truly amazing: She walked me into the nurse's office and demanded that the nurse apologize to me personally too.

The nurse did. She acknowledged that what she did was unprofessional and wrong, and she never lined up students like that ever, ever again. I saved myself and all my friends from further embarrassment. I also gained a whole new respect for speaking up. When it works, other people can really surprise you... even people who seem totally out of your league.

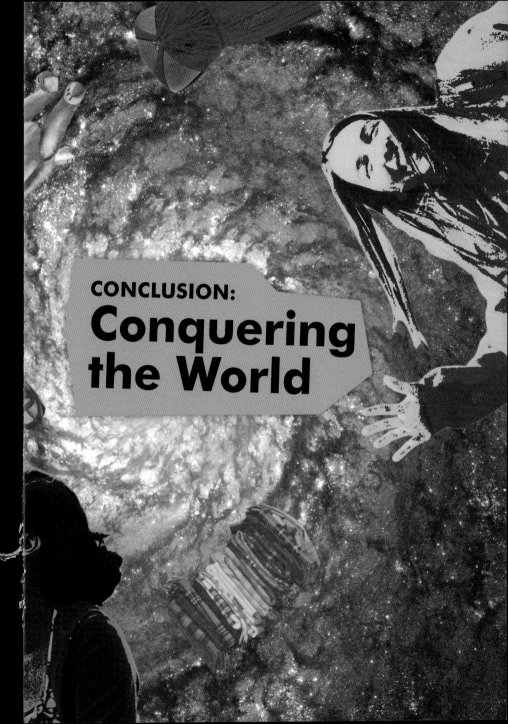

CONCLUSION:
Conquering the World

Middle school can feel like the beginning of so many things:

It's the beginning of your teenage years, the beginning of you starting to make more and more decisions for yourself, and the beginning of discovering who you want be as an adult.

Speaking up is always important, and it's never too late to start. (Some of us don't really start speaking up until we're adults, after all!) But as early as you enter high school, kids begin to work, join political campaigns, volunteer more, and fight for what they believe in. After that, they might be in college, traveling the world, or starting a career or even a family! These things may sound distant and scary, but they're a lot easier to tackle if you approach them with a Speak Up attitude! Now, in middle school, is a *great* time to start learning how to identify your feelings, speak up, and make important changes.

For so many generations, and for so many reasons, young girls your age haven't been able to speak up. I didn't. I couldn't. When I was in middle school, nobody talked about things like self-confidence or gender gaps. Nobody told me that I should speak up or that what I had to say was worth saying.

Instead, as my generation grew up, many of us scrambled to learn basic skills like asking our bosses for raises, asking for what we wanted in relationships with family and friends, or negotiating with a coworker. Some of us are still trying to learn those things, and unfortunately, some of us never will.

You, however, are different. Today, our culture is starting to recognize the obstacles we've put in the way of girls, and we're starting to remove them. It might seem crazy to you that someone who didn't fight a bully used to be called a wimp, and a girl who liked to play sports was called butch. Your generation is more comfortable than ever with being who you are and standing up for what you believe in. You're headed in the right direction, and I hope that what I've shared with you in this book will help you keep going in that direction, full steam ahead.

Right now, if you value speaking up to your friends, family, teachers, bullies, and crushes — whomever you encounter — you can potentially change the future for women. By speaking up, you're changing the way people see you and the way they see themselves. You're changing the world.

I can't wait to see you and your peers totally running things.

Don't ever stop raising your hand.

Further Reading & Resources

- Bazelon, Emily. *Sticks and Stones: Defeating the Culture of Bullying and Rediscovering the Power of Character and Empathy*. Random House, 2013.

  Journalist Emily Bazelon spent years researching this deep-dive into bullying culture in schools. The book defines bullying both in person and online, and explains how adults can combat it.

- The Bully Project. Web. http://www.thebullyproject.com/.

  The Bully Project released BULLY, a documentary film directed by Sundance and Emmy-award winning filmmaker, Lee Hirsch.

- Bullying Statistics. Web. http://www.bullyingstatistics.org/.

  A comprehensive website about bullying, including information and statistics on cyberbullying, gay bullying, bullying laws, and more.

- Cartoon Network. "Stop Bullying: Speak Up." Web. http://www.cartoonnetwork.com/promos/stopbullying/index.html.

  Cartoon Network launched "Stop Bullying: Speak Up" to encourage young people to take an active stand against bullying.

- Child Welfare Information Gateway. Web. https://www.childwelfare.gov/.

  A government website with information on strengthening families and preventing abuse.

- Criswell, Patti Kelley. *A Smart Girl's Guide: Friendship Troubles: Dealing with fights, being left out & the whole popularity thing*. American Girl, 2013.

- Degeneres, Ellen. #UnitedAgainstBullying. Web. http://www.ellentv.com/tags/UnitedAgainstBullying/.

  Ellen Degeneres' #UnitedAgainstBullying campaign site has many videos of famous people speaking out against bullying.

- Holyoke, Nancy. *A Smart Girl's Guide: Boys: Surviving Crushes, Staying True to Yourself, and other (love) stuff*. American Girl, 2014.

  A fun guide for girls who want to start dating. Holyoke includes everything from first-date tips to accounts from real girls, yet the book's primary focus is about maintaining self esteem throughout your dating life.

- Human Rights Campaign: Coming Out. Web. http://www.hrc.org/resources/category/coming-out.

  The Human Rights Campaign: Coming Out provides guidance and resources for lesbian, gay, transgender, bisexual, and questioning youth about coming out.

- Kaufman, Gershen, Lev Raphael, and Pamela Espeland. *Stick Up for Yourself: Every Kid's Guide to Personal Power & Positive Self-Esteem*. Free Spirit, 1999.

  A great resource for kids who need tips on standing up for themselves, whether in a bullying situation at school, or in disagreements at home.

- Moss, Wendy L. *Being Me: A Kid's Guide to Boosting Confidence and Self-Esteem*. Magination, 2010.

  Psychologist and expert Wendy Moss offers tips on building self-confidence. Includes anecdotes from real kids, as well as helpful tips for getting through almost any situation.

- PBS Kids. "It's My Life." Web. http://pbskids.org/itsmylife/index.html.

  A hub for young kids and teens to get information, share stories, take quizzes and polls, and watch videos on topics relevant in their own lives. The site also features celebrity interviews and offers advice from older teens who have been there as well. "It's My Life" is organized into six channels: Friends, Family, School, Body, Emotions, and Money.

- Perlstein, Linda. *Not Much Just Chillin': The Hidden Lives of Middle Schoolers*. Ballantine Books, 2004.

  Journalist Linda Perlstein spent years following middle school kids from various backgrounds in suburban Maryland. Not Much Just Chillin' paints a vivid picture of their inner lives, their desires, and a culture that has befuddled adults for decades.

- "Resources." Pacer's National Bullying Prevention Center. Web. http://www.pacer.org/bullying/resources/, http://www.pacerteensagainstbullying.org/.

  The Pacer Center provides exercises and information about bullying, including ways that kids can prevent bullying within their schools.

- Sandberg, Sheryl. *Lean In: Women, Work, and the Will To Lead*. Knopf, 2013.

  Unfortunately, the challenges of speaking up aren't limited to grade school. They may follow you to college, and eventually, to the workplace. Facebook executive Sheryl Sandberg wrote this inspired book to point out the issues women face at work, and to demonstrate that speaking up — or leaning in — is the key to getting ahead.

- Stomp Out Bullying. Web. http://stompoutbullying.org/.

  Stomp Out Bullying is focused on eliminating bullying and cyber-bullying.

- The Trevor Project. Web. http://www.thetrevorproject.org.

  The Trevor Project provides crisis intervention and suicide prevention for lesbian, gay, transgender, and questioning youth. For immediate help, call their 24- hour hotline: 1-866-488-7386.

- Zelinger, Laurie. *A Smart Girl's Guide to Liking Herself, Even on the Bad Days*. American Girl, 2012.

  Child psychologist Laurie Zelinger uses self-esteem boosters and tips to help girls get through their toughest days.

Acknowledgements

I'd like to thank middle school muses Alexandra Ortiz Stevens, Crystal Raines, Rachel Warner, Caitlin Yang, Katie Murray, & Cheyenne Archer for giving me insight into their minds and lives for the making of this book.

About the Contributors

Halley Bondy is a Brooklyn-based writer. She currently works as a senior producer at Oxygen Networks, and has freelanced for MTV, *Village Voice*, *Vice*, and Red Bull Music Studios. She previously has worked as senior editor for MTV World, and as a news reporter for the *Newark Star Ledger* and *Back Stage*. She is a playwright and comedian, and the winner of the 2008 Fringe Festival NYC for Outstanding Playwright. She is the author of *Don't Sit on the Baby: The Ultimate Babysitting Guide* (2012) and *77 Things You Absolutely Have To Do Before You Finish College* (2014).

Jordyn Bonds has been making collages since high school. In addition to obsessively cutting up magazines, she can be found playing drums and designing interfaces for web and mobile apps.